A Critical Pedagogy of Resistance

TRANSGRESSIONS: CULTURAL STUDIES AND EDUCATION

Cultural studies provides an analytical toolbox for both making sense of educational practice and extending the insights of educational professionals into their labors. In this context *Transgressions: Cultural Studies and Education* provides a collection of books in the domain that specify this assertion. Crafted for an audience of teachers, teacher educators, scholars and students of cultural studies and others interested in cultural studies and pedagogy, the series documents both the possibilities of and the controversies surrounding the intersection of cultural studies and education. The editors and the authors of this series do not assume that the interaction of cultural studies and education devalues other types of knowledge and analytical forms. Rather the intersection of these knowledge disciplines offers a rejuvenating, optimistic, and positive perspective on education and educational institutions. Some might describe its contribution as democratic, emancipatory, and transformative. The editors and authors maintain that cultural studies helps free educators from sterile, monolithic analyses that have for too long undermined efforts to think of educational practices by providing other words, new languages, and fresh metaphors. Operating in an interdisciplinary cosmos, Transgressions: Cultural Studies and Education is dedicated to exploring the ways cultural studies enhances the study and practice of education. With this in mind the series focuses in a non-exclusive way on popular culture as well as other dimensions of cultural studies including social theory, social justice and positionality, cultural dimensions of technological innovation, new media and media literacy, new forms of oppression emerging in an electronic hyperreality, and postcolonial global concerns. With these concerns in mind cultural studies scholars often argue that the realm of popular culture is the most powerful educational force in contemporary culture. Indeed, in the twenty-first century this pedagogical dynamic is sweeping through the entire world. Educators, they believe, must understand these emerging realities in order to gain an important voice in the pedagogical conversation.

Without an understanding of cultural pedagogy's (education that takes place outside of formal schooling) role in the shaping of individual identity--youth identity in particular--the role educators play in the lives of their students will continue to fade. Why do so many of our students feel that life is incomprehensible and devoid of meaning? What does it mean, teachers wonder, when young people are unable to describe their moods, their affective affiliation to the society around them. Meanings provided young people by mainstream institutions often do little to help them deal with their affective complexity, their difficulty negotiating the rift between meaning and affect. School knowledge and educational expectations seem as anachronistic as a ditto machine, not that learning ways of rational thought and making sense of the world are unimportant.

But school knowledge and educational expectations often have little to offer students about making sense of the way they feel, the way their affective lives are shaped. In no way do we argue that analysis of the production of youth in an electronic mediated world demands some "touchy-feely" educational superficiality.

What is needed in this context is a rigorous analysis of the interrelationship between pedagogy, popular culture, meaning making, and youth subjectivity. In an era marked by youth depression, violence, and suicide such insights become extremely important, even life saving. Pessimism about the future is the common sense of many contemporary youth with its concomitant feeling that no one can make a difference.

If affective production can be shaped to reflect these perspectives, then it can be reshaped to lay the groundwork for optimism, passionate commitment, and transformative educational and political activity. In these ways cultural studies adds a dimension to the work of education unfilled by any other sub-discipline. This is what Transgressions: Cultural Studies and Education seeks to produce—literature on these issues that makes a difference. It seeks to publish studies that help those who work with young people, those individuals involved in the disciplines that study children and youth, and young people themselves improve their lives in these bizarre times.

A Critical Pedagogy of Resistance

34 Pedagogues We Need to Know

Edited by

James D. Kirylo
Southeastern Louisiana University, USA

SENSE PUBLISHERS
ROTTERDAM/BOSTON/TAIPEI

A C.I.P. record for this book is available from the Library of Congress.

ISBN: 978-94-6209-372-0 (paperback)
ISBN: 978-94-6209-373-7 (hardback)
ISBN: 978-94-6209-374-4 (e-book)

Published by: Sense Publishers,
P.O. Box 21858,
3001 AW Rotterdam,
The Netherlands
https://www.sensepublishers.com/

Printed on acid-free paper

For
Walter John
Maria Christina
John James

My voice is in tune with a different language, another kind of music. It speaks of resistance, indignation, the just anger of those who are deceived and betrayed. It speaks, too, of their right to rebel against the ethical transgressions of which they are the long-suffering victims.

Paulo Freire

TABLE OF CONTENTS

FOREWORD

LUIS MIRÓN

RADICALIZING DEMOCRACY

A Critical Pedagogy of Resistance: 34 Pedagogues We Need to Know is an ambitious undertaking. James Kirylo's narrative enterprise, which seeks to chronicle the present lives, and those who have passed away of transformative educators (my phrase) is a project whose time has come. I take this phrase not in its idiomatic sense of a "timely book"; but rather in historicizing the present moment of seizing the discursive spaces of education and political agency to take dead aim at the dissolution of global social ills "gone local."

What do I mean by the last statement? On the surface it's readily apparent that inequality of all sorts—social, economic, and yes racial/ethnic—have markedly increased in the past decade, although at least in the US context, the wealth of the middle class has trended consistently downward since the 1970s. For example, in the US there are more back males in the criminal justice system than there are students in college.[1] And the poverty rate among children has reached a staggering 16 million. Nearly 50 million Americans representing 16% of the population is poor.[2]

Extracted globally the percentage increases in hunger, poverty, and populations either homeless or living in squalor have reached frightening proportions. These are not merely the purview of so-called "third world" nations or countries in the southern cone. Indeed cultural and geo-politically advanced industrial societies are similarly characterized. For example Spain has an overall unemployment rate approaching 25%, and among youth the percentage unemployed exceeds 54%.

So, to pose the proverbial questions: What can be done? What do we do? Let's begin with Kirylo's project. I want to start with a few simple, though I hope helpful, distinctions.

For conceptual heuristic purposes, I want to distinguish among the following critical strategies: armed resistance, armed loved, and civic occupation.[3] Camus (1961) wrote passionately both in literary and journalistic genres about the French resistance to Nazi Germany, as well as the human suffering in his native Algeria. He spoke out "in the service of truth and the service of freedom" (p. vii). Clearly armed resistance—French soldiers bearing weapons—are necessary for "love" to have any real meaning in the context of military totalitarianism and slaughter. But resistance need not take militaristic overtones. Following Freire, the concept of *armed love* denotes the passionate—emotionally violent—sensibility, and deployment, of love in the service of social justice. Here the modifier "armed" clearly refers to the metaphorical as distinct from the literal use of arms. The passionate commitment to justice, the use of military and revolutionary arms notwithstanding, however, remains equally intense—if not surpassing armed resistance. Put differently passive resistance and non-violent revolution in the spirit of Mahatma Gandhi, Cesar Chavez, and Martin Luther King come to my mind.

Finally, civic occupation brings in to the present the social practices of critical pedagogy as a means to accomplish social change on the terrain of everyday life. I look to the *Occupy Wall Street* as a guiding social force. Conceived as a loosely-organized protest movement designed to "shut down" Wall Street by literally occupying public spaces during the height of the financial meltdown—"we are the 99%"—this nascent but growing, social movement carries in my judgment a potentially powerful capacity to enact social change by making visible the growing inequalities in the advanced capitalists societies such as the US and the EU. What can we learn from all of these sources of inspiration?

First, from Cesar Chavez the Chicano political chant, *Si se puede*. For in the 2012 U.S. national elections perhaps more so than during President Obama's first election, progressives witnessed the generative possibilities of grassroots politics brought to life. The effect of this movement was captured most vividly by archconservative Governor Bobby Jindal's colorful phrase, [Republicans] need to "stop being the stupid party."[4] Whether or not one agrees with the policies and organizing strategies of the Democratic Party, one fact comes to light: forced pragmatically to choose between two visions of America embodied in two presidential candidates, the nation's Electoral College brought home an electoral landside in the name of narrowing—not widening—inequality of all demographic and ideological stripes. In the lexicon of the 2012 national election it was a victory for the 99% over the champions of the 1% in the likes of Republican governors and former governors such as Bobby Jindal and Mitt Romney.

Shortly after Barack Obama became the first African-American to win the presidency, I published an article somewhat critical of Obama's pragmatism, especially when it came to making cabinet-level appointments (Mirón, 2009). He seemed to rely on the "Chicago crowd" and former president Bill Clinton's constituency. These early moves did not bode well for the high hopes many of us had. Now after the second election I am still not satisfied with the president's policies, for example failure to pass a comprehensive immigration bill and compromising away the single-payer option for *Obamacare*.[5] Perhaps because I have spent the previous five years in administration, I have come to realize the serious constraints on leadership. It is damned hard to make decisions that are progressive as distinct from regressive, redistributive rather than merely distributive of scarce resources. I consider such development to be a less idealistic vision—though this seems to contradict the possibilities of hope—, ironically, however, as enacting a more lasting and sustainable social change. Although this incremental return to democracy falls short of the broader societal aim of critical pedagogy to transform electoral politics into an increase in radical democratic social practices (Carr, 2013 forthcoming, Darder & Mirón, 2006), fundamental movement toward this aim is evident.

My desire and that of my colleague and friend, James Kirylo, is that this ironic twist[6] will not morph into deep skepticism or cynicism, but rather evolve into an aesthetic that as Kierkegaard believed exercised power for the common good.

NOTES

[1] http://m.good.is/posts/new-report-puts-the-black-male-achievement-crisis-in-the-spotlight
[2] http://halfinten.org/issues/families/
[3] I do not wish to conflate, or confuse, "civic occupation" (my term) with civil disobedience or civil unrest/protest.
[4] http://www.politico.com/news/stories/1112/83743.html
[5] I use this term as a synonym for the Affordable Health Care Act without disparagement. Indeed during the presidential debates, the president said that he liked the term.
[6] See Christy Wampole, "How to Live Without Irony." *New York Times* November 18, 2012, p. SR 1.

REFERENCES

Camus, A. (1961). *Resistance, rebellion, and death* (Trans. J. O'Brien). New York: Alfred A. Knopf.
Carr, P. (2013, forthcoming). *Critical pedagogy and democracy*. New York: Peter Lang.
Darder, A., & Mirón L. (2006). Critical pedagogy in a time of uncertainty. *Cultural Studies-Critical Methodologies, 6*(1), 5–20.
Mirón (2009). Ending a nightmare, beginning a dream: Reflections on the outcomes of the election. *Cultural studies-critical methodologies, 9*(6), 793–795.

ACKNOWLEDGMENTS

Book projects are never a solitary event, but rather a process shared by a community. In this case, I am grateful to Shirley Steinberg who without her support this book would have never materialized. I am also very thankful to Michel Lokhorst from Sense Publishers who embraced this project, and Jolanda Karada who nicely guided me to getting this book completed. I am indebted to all the chapter contributors who not only did a commendable job on each of their respective chapters, but who were also great to work with. To all of them, my heartfelt thanks for their expertise, time, and energy. I appreciate the work and thought of Luis Mirón. I am proud to call him colleague and friend, and thank him for writing the FOREWORD. To Dayne Sherman, insightful thinker, activist, and writer, who through our continuous dialogues over the years has been immeasurable. I sincerely thank David Armand, a notable creative writer and author. He always has good ideas, and I very much appreciate his support. And most importantly, to my wonderful wife, Anette, and my two "tesoros," Antonio and Alexander. I am extraordinarily blessed.

JAMES D. KIRYLO

INTRODUCTION

Resistance, Courage, and Action

The history of the human family is fashioned with a potpourri of interesting, exhilarating, and disturbing events. There have been the highest of highs with rudimentary discoveries such as capturing the creative ways of how the flames of fire can be used to the advent of the wheel to the modern miracle of medical advancements to the incredible ever-rapid progress of technology and, most wonderfully, to the realization of how humankind demonstrates profound love for one another through acts of great kindness, compassionate service, and heroic sacrifice.

And then there have been the ongoing conflicts, frustrations, and the lowest of lows. Whether it be addressing the continuing conundrum of making peaceful and just sense between Israel and its middle eastern neighbors to our dealing with the continual repercussions of the ill-advised invasion of Iraq to confronting religious zealots of any stripe who harm and tyrannize, to calling out political leaders who utilize power to corrupt, to critically questioning economic systems that structurally exploit groups of people, to going against the tide of cultural and social mores that marginalize and alienate, to standing against loathsome attitudes and practices that are racist, prejudicial, patriarchal, and discriminatory, to challenging educational systems that systematically leave some in and some out, the human family— seemingly inherently—is in a constant mode of conflict and strife.

As we stand back and examine the human condition, it is naturally a good thing to affirm and celebrate our goodness, intelligence, and innovation, and it is also ethically responsible to scrutinize, challenge, and oppose people, structures, and systems that oppress and dehumanize. Particularly with respect to the latter, enter in critical pedagogy.

The notion of critical pedagogy as a recognized concept is a relatively new phenomenon that particularly emerged from the thought of Paulo Freire and others (McLaren, 2000; Kincheloe, 2008b); however, the consciousness of it as a way of thinking and acting has been around through the ages. When we look back in time where oppressive powers of any kind were at work, human beings have resisted. For example, if we explore the Exodus story, it is one of a people resisting the dominant group, or if we research the life of Bartolomé de Las Casas, who in the mid-1500s, was a powerful voice for the rights of indigenous populations during the barbaric invasion of the conquistadors and colonial Christendom in Latin America, or if we study Fredrick Douglass, who in the 1800s escaped from slavery, which enabled him—through his perceptive intelligence, inspirational oratory skills, and commitment to equality—to devote his life's work toward eradicating slavery, the oppression of women, and injustice of any kind, or if we consider the work of Erich Fromm who, during much of the 20th century, blended his thought through the prism of spirituality, psychology, education, and social theory to challenge demagoguery and to promote the possibilities of hope and authentic human freedom, or if we pay close attention to one of the founders of feminist thought, Susan B Anthony, who was an influential leader during the 19th century in promoting the rights of women, powerfully advocating for equality and justice in the midst of patriarchal structures. Throughout time, whether those dehumanizing forces perpetuated slavery, racism, patriarchy, bigotry or any number of oppressive, exploitive and unjust practices, groups of people responded and courageous leaders emerged with bold voices with what Freire (2005) refers to as a proclamation of denouncing injustice while simultaneously announcing for a more just world.

To be sure, people of justice, people who resist are framed by a vision that embraces an inclusive, tolerant, more loving community that passionately calls for a more democratic citizenship. Freire (2005) puts it this way,

> Citizenship implies freedom—to work, to eat, to dress, to wear shoes, to sleep in a house, to support oneself and one's family, to love, to be angry, to cry, to protest, to support, to move, to participate in this or that religion, this or that party, to educate oneself and one's family, to swim regardless in what ocean of one's country. Citizenship is not obtained by chance: It is a construction that, never finished, demands we fight for it. It demands commitment, political clarity, coherence, decision. (p. 161)

As Freire discernibly suggests, being in the world implies equal opportunity to participate in its movement, which is a central idea in the construct of critical pedagogy. That is, as Macedo (2006) argues, the concept of critical pedagogy is a continuous unfolding process of becoming, where we are active participants that not only includes an ongoing process of encountering pain and struggle, but also a space that is comprised of "hope and joy shaped and maintained by a humanizing pedagogy" (p. 394).

REPRESENTED CRITICAL PEDAGOGUES

The diverse range of critical pedagogues presented in this book comes from a variety of backgrounds with respect to race, gender, and ethnicity, from various geographic places and eras, and from an array of complex political, historical, religious, theological, social, cultural, and educational circumstances which necessitated their leadership and resistance. How each pedagogue uniquely lives in that tension of dealing with pain and struggle, while concurrently fostering a pedagogy that is humanizing, is deeply influenced by their individual autobiographical lens of reality, the conceptual thought that enlightened them, the circumstances that surrounded them, and the conviction that drove them. This underscores Kincheloe's (2008a) assertion that the continuous evolution of critical pedagogy is informed by multiple discourses and is dictated by historical circumstances, new theoretical insights and new challenges, problems, and social situations. In other words, critical pedagogy is an empowering way of thinking and acting, fostering decisive agency that does not take a position of neutrality in its contextual examination of the various forces that impact the human condition. And, in particular, when repressive forces are at work dehumanizing, oppressing, and marginalizing people, critical pedagogues are those who emerge as powerful humanizing agents to resist and call for a more just, right, and democratic world. That is just what the 34 critical pedagogues represented in this text heroically do.

Throughout the world, there are, of course, hundreds of well-known and not so well-known critical pedagogues from across a variety of disciplines and experiences who have significantly contributed to critical thought and action. It is thusly obvious that volumes can be written about the variety of critical pedagogues who have appeared on the scene over the ages. Notwithstanding the pre-defined space limitations authors are typically allocated, a challenge of producing a text such as this was determining who should be included, a task that naturally took some thoughtful consideration. The idea behind that consideration was not so much of a fear of who would be left out (that was an unavoidable given), but, rather an imaginative vision of who would be included and whom would well represent a critical pedagogy of resistance from a variety of contexts, circumstances, and points of view, while also representing the numerous critical pedagogues who do not appear here. So the number 34 was not a predetermined magic figure of how many pedagogues would be included; rather, 34 was the natural stopping point at which, to reiterate, seems to collectively exemplify the face of a critical pedagogy of resistance.

The following are the critical pedagogues represented in the book: Michael Apple, Stanley Aronowitz, Lilia Bartolomé, Deborah Britzman, Judith Butler, Noam Chomsky, Antonia Darder, John Dewey, W.E.B. Du Bois, Michael E. Dyson, Ignacio Ellacuría, Ana Maria Araújo Freire, Paulo Freire, Henry Louis Gates, Jr., Carol Gilligan, Henry Giroux, Jesus "Pato" Gomez, Antonio Gramsci, bell hooks, Myles Horton, Ivan Illich, Joe Kincheloe, Alfie Kohn, Jonathan Kozol, Donaldo Macedo, Peter McLaren, Maria Montessori, Edward Saïd, Ira Shor, Shirley Steinberg, Aung San Suu Kyi, Lev Vygotsky, Simone Weil, and Cornel West. From examining these various individuals, it is clear that all have in one way or another lived, experienced, or observed oppressive forces at work, prompting all of them in their own unique ways to speak out, to act, to push back, and to resist. Within that examination of the highlighted pedagogues, it also appears that two groups of individuals loosely emerge. There is one group in which its members personally experienced and lived under terrifying and dangerous oppressive circumstances whereby their very lives were threatened (as in the case of Paulo Freire, Aung San Suu Kyi, and others), and even taken out (as in the case of Ignacio Ellacuría), and another group who has lived (and continues to do so) under a constant cloud of losing their jobs, status, and the distorting of reputation for taking positions of resistance. Yet they all audaciously remain in the struggle of calling out powerful, well-financed entities that make every attempt to marginalize their thought.

I am reminded of the Brazilian theologians Leonardo and Clodovis Boff, both of whom significantly contributed to the thought of liberation theology and the concept of "preferential option for the poor." In their work *Liberation theology: From Dialogue to Confrontation* (1986), they discuss that there are three ways to demonstrate a commitment to the poor: (a) visiting the poor; (b) conducting scholarly research, writing, and teaching about the living conditions of the poor; and (c) permanently living among the poor. Taking my cue, therefore, from Boff and Boff and applying the same strand of thinking that guided their thought, all the critical pedagogues highlighted in this text, in one way or another, have monumentally demonstrated their commitment to justice and a more right world by (a) regularly visiting blighted communities and immersing themselves in the struggle to speak out against tyrannical thought of any kind; (b) writing, researching, and teaching the political, social, economic, and education conditions that enable injustice, and what can be done to thwart those toxic conditions; and, (c) permanently living in shattered communities or circumstances in an effort to be an instrument of service and a light of hope toward facilitating a more humanizing reality. In the final analysis, all of the highlighted critical pedagogues collectively stand in solidarity with all peoples who have been given what Kincheloe (1992) describes as the "short end of the historical stick" and "have not found their way into the 'official' story" (p. 644).

Moreover, as one explores this text, s/he will also discover a common disposition that is woven throughout the lives of all the represented pedagogues. First, each is clearly driven by an unwavering conviction to promoting justice and democratic spaces; second, each in their own unique way possesses a deep love for humanity; third, each is guided by a strong sense of hope for a better today and tomorrow; and, finally, most of the contemporary critical pedagogues herein have been linked or influenced by the work of Paulo Freire. Particularly with respect to the latter, Freire's impact on the thinking of many featured in this text cannot be overstated: his general influence on educational, philosophical, and theological thought has been nothing short of remarkable, marking him as one of the most important educators the world has seen in the last 100 years. Perhaps Torres (1982) best captures the point when he declares, "We can stay with Freire or against Freire, but not without Freire" (p. 94).

WHERE DO WE GO FROM HERE?

John Dewey, W.E.B. Du Bois, Ignacio Ellacuría, Paulo Freire, Jesus "Pato" Gomez, Antonio Gramsci, Myles Horton, Ivan Illich, Joe Kincheloe, Maria Montessori, Edward Saïd, Lev Vygotsky, and Simone Weil are no longer with us, but their theories of critical thought significantly remain. They challenge us to continue our movement forward in order to build a world that promotes authentic freedom and equal opportunity for all. And challenges remain. The work of Michael Apple, Stanley Aronowitz, Lilia Bartolomé, Deborah Britzman, Judith Butler, Noam Chomsky, Antonia Darder, Michael E. Dyson, Ana Maria Araújo Freire, Henry Louis Gates, Jr., Carol Gilligan, Henry Giroux, bell hooks, Alfie Kohn, Jonathan Kozol, Donaldo Macedo, Peter McLaren, Ira Shor, Shirley Steinberg, Aung San Suu Kyi, and Cornel West continues to tirelessly confront those challenges as, indeed, all of us should necessarily do in our own ways.

Steinberg (2007) reminds us that an aspect of critical pedagogy gives us a certain pass to be angry, an anger that calls out "uses of power and at injustices through the violations of human rights" (p. ix). Moreover, Freire (2005) makes the salient point that our denunciation of injustice should be framed within what he calls an "armed love" (p. 74). In that traditional space called a classroom, critical educators have a unique responsibility to be mindful that the notion of pedagogy is perpetually joined at the hip with forces related to the economic, social, and political sphere (Giroux, 2007; 2011). And where economic injustice is evident, where violations of human rights are occurring, where equal-access and opportunity have been subverted, and where freedoms have been violated, critical educators should not only examine the impact this has on students and society as a whole, but they should also act with an honorable anger and with what Darder (2002) characterizes as a "pedagogy of love" (p. 30).

We are living in interesting times. That many children around the world are dying from preventable diseases or illnesses (e.g., pneumonia, diarrhea, and other infirmities), exploited on multiple levels (e.g., child labor, forced prostitution, and other disturbing practices), and remain in a state of hunger are all troubling reminders that we have more critical work to do; that we have political parties that can no longer speak to each other, obliterating any kind of impulse of the rightful place of humility, which clearly signals to us that the concept of authentic dialogue continues to be needed at the table; that there is an arsenal of nuclear weapons in possession of various countries, constantly making it clear that the annihilation of the human family is a very real threat if we don't collectively get our act together; that discrimination, prejudice, and bigotry of any kind still exist makes evident we still have work to do in fostering unity in our diversity; and, finally, that the gap between the rich and the rest of us (as Smiley and West (2012) put it) is ever widening, squeezing out even more what is left of the mythical middle class, should provide a clarion call to challenge economic systems that exploit and systematically leave some of us in and a whole lot of us out. And the particular threat that is leaving a whole lot of us out is driven by an avalanche of neoliberal thought.

Largely backed by corporate capital in advancing its point of view, neoliberalism possesses an ideology that promotes privatization, individualism, competition, and profit, all of which are having a disturbing impact on dismantling anything public, and even calling into question the survival of our very democracy and that critical space called the public square. Giroux (2011) makes the point that neoliberalism cultivates a way of thinking and acting whereby "...the language of the social is either devalued or ignored altogether as the idea of the public sphere is equated with a predatory space rife with danger and disease—as in reference to public restrooms, public transportation, and urban public schools. Dreams of the future are now modeled around the narcissistic, privatized, and self-indulgent needs of consumer culture and the dictates of the alleged free market" (p. 112).

Particularly with respect to education, a neoliberal trajectory can be characterized as the marketization of education whereby students are viewed as commodities, teachers as mechanical functionaries, and the primary purpose of schooling is singularly tied to the economic growth of the community (Kirylo, 2013). This marketization views education as a positivistic endeavor, advocating rigid standardization while at the same time dismissing the relevance of cultural sensitivities and developmentally appropriate approaches to teaching and learning. The individual is valued over the group; competition trumps collaboration; self-centeredness outmatches cooperation; and, the notion of the common good has no place. Moreover, this marketization seeks to defund public education through the advocating of vouchers, so-called choice, and corporate takeover of schools. Finally, this marketization of education is working to not only irresponsibly marginalize the purpose and necessity of academic freedom and tenure, but is also working hard to systematically deprofessionalize the notion of teacher education, even advocating for the eradication of its very existence. To be sure, this entire scenario is a very real and present danger that is working to dismantle anything public. All of this should grab our collective attention simply because if we allow this course to continue, we will see more power handed over to the few who already possess the majority of it; we will see the furthering of the economic divide; and, we will see the continual erosion of authentic democratic participation.

RESISTANCE, COURAGE, ACTION

In light of the entire reality described above, where do we go from here? We not only reinvent Freire's thought and work within our own circumstances, but we realize as Steinberg (2007) suggests that "critical pedagogy takes language from the radical—radicals must do" (p. ix). We must all actively remain immersed in our communities, our realities, and where injustice is perpetrated we need to resist, take courage, and act.

REFERENCES

Boff, L., & Boff, C. (1986). *Liberation theology: From dialogue to confrontation* (R. R. Barr, Trans.). San Francisco, CA: Harper & Row.

Darder, A. (2002). *Reinventing Paulo Freire: A pedagogy of love*. Boulder, CO: Westview Press.

Freire, P. (2005). *Teachers as cultural workers: Letters to those who dare teach* (expanded edition). Boulder, CO: Westview Press.

Giroux, H. A. (2011). *On critical pedagogy*. New York, NY: Continuum.

Giroux, H. A. (2007). Introduction: Democracy, education, and the politics of critical pedagogy. In P. McLaren & J. L. Kincheloe, *Critical pedagogy: Where are we now?* (pp. 1–5). New York, NY: Peter Lang.

Kincheloe, J. L. (2008a). *Critical pedagogy* (2nd ed.). Peter Lang Primer. New York, NY: Peter Lang.

Kincheloe, J. L. (2008b, Spring–Summer). Afterward: Ten short years—Acting on Freire's Requests. *Journal of Thought, 43*(1&2), 163–171.

Kincheloe, J. L. (1992, October). Liberation theology and the attempt to establish an emancipatory system of meaning. Paper presented at the Bergamo Conference on Curriculum Theory and Classroom Practice, Dayton, OH. In W. Pinar, W. Reynolds, P. Slattery, & P. Taubman, *Understanding curriculum* (pp. 606–660). New York, NY: Peter Lang.

Kirylo, J. (2013). Introduction: Critical pedagogy in an age of the marketization of education. In L. M. Christensen & J. Aldridge, *Critical pedagogy for early childhood and elementary educators* (pp. 1–4). New York: Springer.

Macedo, D. (2006). *Literacies of power: What Americans are not allowed to know.* Boulder, CO: Westview Press.

McLaren, P. (2000). *Che Guevara, Paulo Freire, and the pedagogy of revolution.* Lanham MD: Rowman & Littlefield Publishers, Inc.

Smiley, T., & West, C. R. (2012). *The rich and the rest of us: A poverty manifesto.* New York: SmileyBooks.

Steinberg, S. R. (2007). Preface: Where are we now? In P. McLaren & J. L. Kincheloe, *Critical pedagogy: Where are we now?* (pp. ix–x). New York, NY: Peter Lang.

Torres, C. A. (1982). From the pedagogy of the oppressed to a luta continua – An essay on the political pedagogy of Paulo Freire. *Education with Production Review, 2,* 76–97.

AIM OF BOOK

The aim of this book is threefold. First, the highlighting of the variety of critical pedagogues is intended to not only serve as a springboard to engage us in dialogue about pivotal issues and concerns related to justice, equality, and opportunity, but also to hopefully lead us to further explore deeper into the lives and thought of some extraordinary people. In fact, it is worthy to point out that this text is unique in the sense that the diverse group of individuals discussed represents a variety of disciplines, points-of-view, and who have lived (or are currently living) in varying eras, yet all of them should necessarily fall under the umbrella of being characterized as critical pedagogues. To state another way, there are represented individuals highlighted in this text who are not "educators" or "teachers" in the conventional connotation and still others who may not be viewed conventionally as critical pedagogues, and, finally there are those who have been highlighted whom one would logically expect to see in a text such as this. Yet, despite that diversity, all of them have in common a distinctive story that can powerfully, uniquely, and contemporarily teach us in collectively processing dilemmas, questions, and concerns of the social, political, education, and cultural order.

Second, the intent of this book is to affirm and challenge our own thinking. That is, through the work of the highlighted critical pedagogues, a variety of themes are explored which are linked to education, race, ethnicity, gender, theology, language, power, and justice, among other topics. All of us naturally have a certain lens of the world, and there will likely be aspects in this text that will comfortably affirm that lens; however, there also may be some strands of thought articulated that may take us out of our comfort zone and challenge us, which hopefully will lead to deeper reflection into and exploration of our personal worldview.

Finally, the aim of this book is to inspire. Indeed, the ultimate goal of a teacher is to inspire. Inspiration inevitably prompts us to think, to move, to act. Through the remarkable lives and thought of the cross-section of critical pedagogues highlighted in this book, the hope is that we are all moved to continue the work of making a more just, right, and democratic world.

A WORD ABOUT THE CHAPTER CONTRIBUTORS

The diverse range of chapter/co-chapter contributors who earnestly participated in this project come from various parts of the world. For some, English is their second or third language, which is quite impressive because of the necessary skill, time, and commitment that is needed, particularly when working with technical or content-related vocabulary and concepts. While there are some format similarities within all of the chapters, each contributor, however, was naturally led by his/her own imagination, writing style, and approach as to what he/she thought was necessary to emphasize in order to capture the essence of the critical pedagogue discussed. Because each contributor was given a limited word count range with which to work, each was challenged in her/his own way to centrally capture the thought and life of their chosen pedagogue. To be sure, many of the critical pedagogues in this book have such notability and presence that there are volumes written about their lives and work, and to somehow succinctly encapsulate that in a confined space takes some creativity. In that light, the chapter contributors must be complimented for their efforts because they each did a tremendous job on that score. Moreover, a nice feature in all of the chapters is the accessible language, style, and approach that was taken which should be appealing to a wide-range audience. This latter point cannot be overstated because it can be demanding to write in a clear and concise way about topics and themes that can be quite complex and multi-nuanced. As a point of reference, the logical ordering of the chapters is simply arranged alphabetically by the critical pedagogue's last name. In the end, all of the chapter contributors did a remarkable job in celebrating and recognizing a group of critical pedagogues we all need to know and who have made a difference in the world.

LYDIAH NGANGA & JOHN KAMBUTU

1. MICHAEL APPLE

A Modern Day Critical Pedagogue

Michael Apple, a professor of educational policy since the early 1970s at the University of Wisconsin-Madison, is internationally recognized for his pioneering work in what has become known as critical pedagogy, a lens from which power and inequality is explored. Because traditional educational practices in the U.S. confer cultural legitimacy to groups in power and privilege while generating and supporting structural inequalities for groups that have been historically disenfranchised, Apple supports an education for social and cognitive awakening.

Apple's interest in critical pedagogy was shaped by his life experiences. In addition to growing up poor, Apple realized the intersection between poverty and educational injustices while teaching in inner city schools. Equally awakening were his experiences as a graduate scholar at Columbia University where he recognized the disconnect between curricula and learners' lived experiences. Consequently, he joined his family's tradition of social activism and struggle for social justice. In particular, Apple questioned the value of an education that did not address social injustices, and grappled with societal labels of "less than" with respect to people in poverty (Apple, 2012a).

EDUCATION IS NOT A NEUTRAL ENTERPRISE

As a critical pedagogue, Apple postulates that traditional education is not neutral. Rather, it is political, designed to advance the interests of the groups in power and privilege (Apple, 2012b). To the extent that education is not neutral, Apple supports educational activism which embraces principles of critical pedagogy whereby rational educators are fully aware of societal power dynamics that illuminates abuses of power, domination, and exploitation, particularly as it relates to curricula practices (Apple 1996). For example, to interrogate curricula practices, Apple (2000) asked educators to seek answers to the following questions: What counts as legitimate knowledge? What knowledge is of most worth? Whose knowledge is of most worth? (p. 44). Unless existing curricula and policies are examined, then education will continue to support an unjust infrastructure.

Because Apple argues that education in the U.S. is unjust, he contends a "them vs. us" mentality is prominent in educational policies and practices. Further, Apple asserts that traditional schooling is designed to control people's thinking

James D. Kirylo (Ed.), A Critical Pedagogy of Resistance: 34 Pedagogues We Need to Know, 1–4.
© *2013 Sense Publishers. All rights reserved.*

and behavior. In other words, U.S. schools possess what can be characterized as knowledge legitimacy, i.e., they decide the curricula to adopt, which is typically a European-based curricula perspective. By assigning Eurocentric canons higher status, other curricula are deemed inferior and of less epistemological value. To reverse this trend, therefore, Apple recommends a systematic critical analysis of educational policies that have guided education in the U.S.

By and large, U.S. education serves the interests of privileged groups. Consequently, it has had a disempowering effect on groups that have been historically disenfranchised (Apple, 2000). To exemplify the point and from a personal perspective, Apple tells of his son, a person of color, undergoing a state of utter powerlessness as a result of unjust school experiences. Yet, not only from a personal point of view and from his own research, Apple asserts that the privileged still believe strongly in the fairness of existing educational policies and practices. Nieto and Bode (2012) make the point that because the privileged have access to multiple resources, they lack critical consciousness relative to the "resource, opportunity and expectation" gaps the underprivileged experience, thus limiting their chances for academic success (p. 13). In that light, Apple recommends an objective analysis of educational practices in the context of sociocultural and sociopolitical/economic factors, and calls for activism against educational systems that reinforce, reproduce and preserve inequalities through curricula and evaluative activities.

Because power influences educational policies and practices, and because he critically questions neoliberal and neoconservative philosophies, Apple supports a restructuring of traditional schooling to create a space for transforming education, one that does not romanticize the notion that "everyone is the same" (Apple, 2004, p. 27). In other words, while people are created equal, they have different lived experiences, ultimately necessitating an education for critical consciousness which is transforming and empowering. Indeed, without critical awareness, people are likely to believe that "things are the way they are because they cannot be otherwise," (Freire, 1997, p. 36). So, like Freire, Apple supports an education that confronts issues of dominance and subornation.

Predictably, Apple's support for an education that challenges the status-quo is resisted by groups in positions of power as was evident in South Korea where he was once arrested. Nevertheless, because Apple believes in the liberating nature of an education for critical consciousness, his work has a global appeal especially in the current context of globalization. To be sure, globalization is influencing educational systems in variety of ways. However, due to increasing global injustices, the notion of a global critical pedagogy possesses its rightful place. As a consequence, Apple challenges educators worldwide to implement transformative education in order to nurture epistemological spaces essential to freedom, democracy and social justice. Additionally, he reminds educators to maintain their movement toward critical consciousness while confronting issues of power and privilege (Apple & Beane, 2007). As Apple (2011) contends, "part of the task of the critical scholar/activist in education is to make public the success in contesting the unequal policies, curricula, pedagogy and evaluation" (p. 29). An education for critical consciousness is essential to the establishment of a more just and equitable society. To Apple, such an education is inclusive. Therefore, it respects the contributions, histories and experiences of all people, both privileged and marginalized. However, because education is political, Apple asserts that educational policies and practices should be scrutinized continually using educational and social justice lens, and in a spirit of collaboration between all stakeholders.

CONCLUSION

Michael Apple is a modern day critical analyst. As an educational theorist who grounds his scholarship in daily struggles for social justice, Apple believes in critical curricula, implemented in democratic spaces. Apple's childhood experiences with injustice heightened his consciousness relative to the intersection between educational practices and social injustices. Therefore, in his quest for a more just world, Apple advocates an education that not only challenges the status quo, but also fosters a way of thinking that is reflectively critical and transformative.

REFERENCES

Apple, M. W. (1996). *Cultural politics and education*. New York: Teachers College Press.
Apple, M. W. (2000). *Official knowledge: Democratic knowledge in a conservative age* (2nd ed.). New York: Routledge.
Apple, M. W. (2004). *Ideology and curriculum* (3rd ed.). New York: Routledge.
Apple, M. W. (2011). Democratic education in neoliberal and neoconservative times. *International Studies in Sociology of Education, 21*(1), 21–31.
Apple, M. W. (2012a). *Can education change society?* New York: Routledge.
Apple, M. W. (2012b). *Knowledge, power, and education: The selected works of Michael W. Apple*. New York: Routledge.
Apple, M. W., & Beane, J. A. (2007). *Democratic schools*. Portsmouth, NH: Heinemann.
Freire, P. (1997). *Pedagogy of the heart*. New York: Continuum.
Nieto, S., & Bode, P. (2012). *Affirming diversity: The sociopolitical context of multicultural education* (6th ed.). Boston, MA: Pearson/Allyn & Bacon.

GABRIEL MORLEY

2. STANLEY ARONOWITZ

Intellectual and Cultural Critic

Stanley Aronowitz is a prominent American leftist scholar who writes widely on issues related to sociology, science, labor, and education. A former New York gubernatorial candidate who ran on the Green Party ticket in 2002, Aronowitz considers his primary role as that of public intellectual and cultural critic. He is commonly considered a leading figure in the critical postmodernist vein along with other radical theorists like Henry Giroux and Peter McLaren. A staunch supporter of the labor movement, Aronowitz began his career as an adult educator organizing for labor unions where he insisted that learning should be practical. Further, he concludes that all education is political and should serve to empower the oppressed.

Aronowitz has been professor of sociology and urban education at the Graduate Center of City University of New York (CUNY) for nearly three decades. In addition to his teaching and research, Aronowitz is also director of the Center for the Study of Culture, Technology and Work at CUNY. Formerly, he taught at the University of California – Irvine and Staten Island Community College. Additionally, Aronowitz was instrumental in founding the academic journal *Social Text*, which examines social and cultural issues around the world. In 2005, he co-founded the journal *Situations: Project of the Radical Imagination*, which attempts to insert imaginative thought into political theory in an attempt to discover new ideas.

Born in 1933 in New York to Jewish working class parents, Aronowitz was inundated from an early age with a working class ethos. He attended public schools in New York until he was enrolled at Brooklyn College where he was promptly suspended for participating in a sit-in. His demonstration against authority continued when he refused to re-enrol at the college after being granted permission by the administration to return to school. Instead, Aronowitz spent the next 15 years primarily working in steel mills and factories around New York and New Jersey. It was during this time he developed strong ties to the labor movement and began to understand the struggle among the social classes in America. Also, during this time, Aronowitz became interested in community organizing and turned his skills toward union work. He traveled the country organizing and educating workers for a variety of labor organizations, including the Amalgamated Clothing Workers and the Oil, Chemical and Atomic Workers' Union. Aronowitz returned to school in the late 1960s and earned an undergraduate degree from the New School in 1968. Seven years later he graduated from Union Graduate School (now Union Institute) with a Ph.D.

James D. Kirylo (Ed.), A Critical Pedagogy of Resistance: 34 Pedagogues We Need to Know, 5–8.

Aronowitz has authored or co-authored 25 books about social class, education, and American culture. His first book, *Honor America: The Nature of Fascism, Historic Struggles Against It and a Strategy for Today*, was published in 1970. Three years later, Aronowitz published *False Promises: the Shaping of American Working Class Consciousness*, a text on the labor movement. *False Promises* was a breakout work for Aronowitz. He gained acclaim for its critical assessment of the unions during the 1960s and 1970s, arguing that union leadership was not leading workers, but instead was focused on being a mouthpiece for mediation to placate employers. Aronowitz urged more radical leadership from union bosses in order to gain more rights for workers.

From his earliest days as an organizer, Aronowitz understood the power of education. As his awareness of the battleground of education policy and practice evolved, Aronowitz began to critique the structure and purpose of schooling. His first book about education, *Education Under Siege* (1985), co-authored with Henry Giroux, examined public school funding and the politics of education. The authors collaborated again a few years later in a follow-up book, *Education Still Under Siege* (1993), which explored the reform changes that had taken place in schools across the country during the period when Ronald Reagan was president. Aronowitz and Giroux (1993) argued that political conservatives had usurped the meaning and purpose of schooling and were privatizing education toward individualism to satisfy corporate capitalism. Essentially, the principles of democracy and civic-mindedness were being replaced in classrooms with a sense of competitiveness and a winner-take-all approach to education. The authors further noted that such conservative reforms are ongoing because radical educators have provided no compelling counter-vision to the conservative push to link business and education.

Expounding upon his argument about the politicization of education, Aronowitz began to look at the effects of a trend in higher education away from the liberal arts toward a more specialized curriculum designed to train students for specific skills or jobs. He viewed this as a continuation of the privatization of schooling in order to meet marketplace demands. In *The Knowledge Factory: Dismantling the Corporate University and Creating True Higher Learning* (2000) Aronowitz expands his critique of education arguing that higher education in America has become less about learning and more akin to vocational training for individuals in order to learn specific skills for private interests. He maintains that this approach to higher education misguides students into thinking that they must comply with corporate authority, establishing an ongoing social structure that is reluctant to challenge the status quo. Instead, Aronowitz encourages colleges and universities to engage students in meaningful critical conversations about social, economic, and political realities that confront systems of power.

Nearly a decade after writing *Education Still Under Siege* (1993), Aronowitz returns to his critique of k-12 schooling in the face of more conservative education reforms implemented during the George Bush presidency, most notably high-stakes testing. Aronowitz (2004) critiques education and schooling because he believes children are being prepared for a life of labor and are being trained by schools to fall into order within the proper cultural, economic, and social classes. He maintains that evidence shows schools are not equitable and do not provide a level playing field for all socioeconomic groups despite claims otherwise. This imbalance renders individuals inert and, therefore, ties them to the same social class they have always known. In reality, Aronowitz (2004) says, there is very little upward mobility within social classes.

In his most current work about education, *Against Schooling: For an Education that Matters* (2008), Aronowitz focuses on what he perceives as the most damaging conservative reform in schooling – high-stakes testing, which is a direct result of increased corporatization of schooling. Standardized testing and the ancillary economic windfall that is coupled with it is clear evidence of the privatization of education, according to Aronowitz. He refutes claims that education needs to be regulated through current *standards* that are determined somewhat indiscriminately by politics and wealthy business interests. Aronowitz posits that schools are no longer enlightening, but have become bureaucratic institutions with the aim of reproducing workers for the ruling class. Interestingly, Aronowitz is able to draw a link between his criticism of labor and education. He notes that most working class children will become less well off than their working class parents because of a drop in the number of industrial jobs, and because of low wages paid to workers as a result of the decline in unionization.

In an attempt to offer a radical challenge to the current educational status quo, Aronowitz (2004) proposes a three-fold reform. First, as a society we need to define our expectations related to education taking into consideration cultural context. Aronowitz feels the current curricula needs to be situated in a social context in order to make it relevant to learners. Second, an overhaul of education schools is needed to reverse the current teacher training methodology. Aronowitz suggests that teachers need to be trained as intellectuals, which requires teacher training based on subject disciplines as opposed to teaching methods. Finally, Aronowitz calls for a movement of people who must insist that schools receive adequate funding and dismiss high-stakes testing. He argues that standardized testing does not work as an assessment tool because it overruns the curriculum and relegates teachers to trainers who merely prepare students for tests.

Aronowitz has spent his career critiquing society, politics, economics, science, and education. He advocates for greater civic participation from individuals and a more intensive focus on democracy at all levels in all endeavors because in his estimation the impetus for social change is situated in shared cultural, economic, and political experiences (Aronowitz, 1992). Changing the structure of schooling, for Aronowitz, is paramount to the success of any future social change.

REFERENCES

Aronowitz, S. (2004). Against schooling: Education and social class. *Workplace, 6*(1).
Aronowitz, S. (2008). *Against schooling: For an education that matters.* Boulder, CO: Paradigm Publishers.

Aronowitz, S. (1992). *False promises: The shaping of American working class consciousness.* Durham, NC: Duke University Press.

Aronowitz, S. (2000). *The knowledge factory: Dismantling the corporate university and creating true higher learning.* Boston, MA: Beacon Press.

Aronowitz, S. & Giroux, H. A. (1985). *Education under siege: The conservative, liberal and radical debate over schooling.* South Hadley, MA: Bergin & Garvey.

Aronowitz, S. & Giroux, H. A. (1993). *Education still under siege.* South Hadley, MA: Bergin & Garvey.

3. LILIA BARTOLOMÉ

Calling Attention to the Ideological Clarity of Teachers

My love of literacy and learning helped to produce a proud Mexicana/Chicana who was serious about her commitment to her community...Life has taught me that solidarity must extend beyond one's particular ethnic group to various groups who share – even more than skin color – past and current experiences of subordination and oppression...Clearly, home and family environments are critical factors in every child's success. Teachers need to free themselves from adhering rigidly to their own methods and work to incorporate students' home experiences into reading pedagogy. My teachers would have learned a tremendous amount if they taken the time to tap into my 'funds of knowledge'... Luckily for me, my family literacy practices and my eventual politicization compensated for the shortcomings of the school.

Bartolomé, 2011, 58–59

The above autobiographical reflection allows one to take a glimpse into the personal and professional life of Lilia Bartolomé, a Professor of Applied Linguistics at the University of Massachusetts in Boston. Bartolomé grew up in a barrio of southeastern San Diego in a bilingual and bicultural family with a mother from Sinaleo, Mexico, and a father with roots in the Philippines. These life experiences nurtured her dedication not only to her ethnic and linguistic community but also to all people who have been historically disenfranchised. Liberation philosophies and critical pedagogies promoted by Paulo Freire, Henry Giroux, Gloria Anzaldua and others shaped Bartolomé's identity and her voice as a progressive Chicana professor with a strong research agenda for fostering multiculturalism. In her works of more than two decades, a strong cohesive theme emerges: the demand for teachers' political and ideological clarity in order to effectively and equitably educate all children, but especially those of a minority status. This chapter offers a synopsis of this theme in light of her works.

MINORITY STUDENTS' RIGHT TO NATIVE LANGUAGE

The achievement and graduation rate of Latino students in the United States is alarmingly low, indicating a major deficiency of the current educational system. Bartolomé critically examines the reasons for this failure and presents

James D. Kirylo (Ed.), A Critical Pedagogy of Resistance: 34 Pedagogues We Need to Know, 9–12.

a multifaceted, historically-embedded analysis of the past and present of the American educational system and society, proposing a well-grounded radical stand about the future. Specifically, based on research evidence about the academic and psychological advantages of bilingual education, she advocates for the right of students to learn in their native language. The native language, which is a crucial component of students' reality, prior experience and background knowledge, should serve as a foundation and a tool in their learning. Moreover, literacy programs should be based on the heritage language so that students can develop their own voice, a positive self-concept, and cultural identity in order to reconstruct their histories and cultures. Thus, Bartolomé urges teachers to become mindful of the cultural and linguistic heritage of children who are considered minorities; moreover, she intensely contends that pure knowledge of 'teacher-proof' strategies is insufficient without the teachers' authentic love (cariño), respect and positive attitude toward students. In particular, effective early childhood programs should offer heritage language instruction saturated with these components – love, respect, and positive attitude – in contrast to English-only instruction (Bartolomé, 1998; 2008a).

Bartolomé also calls attention to the political and ideological contexts of minority education – the widespread English-only legacy – which institutionalizes a racist approach of banning the use of non-English languages and confirms the unjust, asymmetrical power in education. In accordance with Gloria Anzaldua, a Chicana poet and activist, Bartolomé perceives this linguistic assimilation of non-white immigrants more precisely described as *domestication,* because of the broken promise of people of color getting a share of the power, if they give up their native language. Her concern about the English-only legacy is timelier than ever, considering the recent anti-immigration and anti-bilingual movements in states such as Arizona, Alabama, and California. When teachers, policy-makers, and others are cognizant of the consequences of poverty, such as the dehumanizing and oppressive conditions in the lives of children that are minorities, they might understand that the implementation of the English-only programs – pedagogy of exclusion in reality – will not guarantee higher achievement for them. Consequently, Bartolomé demands the deconstruction and reconstruction of the political and ideological aspect of bilingual education, rejecting the notion that bilingual education is strictly a pedagogical issue rather than political and ideological. Because it is essential that teachers develop an understanding of the links between language, power, politics and ideology in schools, she argues for the infusion of critical pedagogy and the study of ideology in teacher preparation courses (Bartolomé, 2006; Bartolomé & Leistyna, 2006).

IDEOLOGY AND TEACHER EDUCATION

Further broadening the scope of her research, Bartolomé comprehensively demands the critical need for examining the ideologies that guide teacher education. When teacher candidates, who are largely white middle class women, unconsciously hold and/or uncover dominant discriminatory ideologies, such as meritocracy, assimilation, and deficit views of students that are oppressed, they are also likely to accept the unequal power distribution in schools and society as natural and unchangeable. This lack of ideological clarity, that is the inability to recognize the historical, economic and social conditions that mold our lives, might lead teachers to exhibit disrespect, unfair treatment, and 'miseducation' toward students that have been historically disenfranchised, ultimately causing harm to their intellectual pursuits and emotional well-being.

Often these teachers, whose performance evaluation might heavily be based on student achievement on standardized tests, blame the students and their culture and language for poor academic attainment instead of critically reflecting on the socio-historical context and the consequences of discriminatory ideologies. Therefore, teacher education programs should necessarily cultivate an environment whereby teacher candidates explicitly scrutinize their own ideological dimensions toward school-aged youngsters, specifically naming and critiquing discriminatory ideologies as well as identifying effective counter-hegemonic orientations. In fact, Bartolomé implemented this theoretical argument in practice by infusing the study of ideology in teacher education courses, and, as a result of this infusion, she observed prospective teachers growing into committed educators of students that are minorities (Bartolomé, 2010).

Bartolomé fiercely dispels the notion that education is mainly a technical issue, asserting that the uncritical replication of methodologies in the spirit of "methods fetish" cannot assure academic growth. Instead, she argues only ideologically clear educators can implement emancipatory and humanizing pedagogy, and that teacher candidates should be empowered with skills for critically selecting culturally and linguistically responsive approaches to instruction (Macedo & Bartolomé, 2001). In other words, Bartolomé makes the case in her research that effective educators recognize that teaching is not an apolitical endeavor, but an ethical and moral undertaking, rejecting the subordinate status of those students who have been classified as minority. To this extent, effective educators are those who act as cultural brokers, mentors, advocates and critical pedagogues for their students, equalizing "the unequal playing field."

To that end, therefore, ideological clarity, ethics, solidarity and courage should serve as four cornerstones in teacher preparation programs. The mission with these four pillars in mind should necessarily be embraced and infused throughout the curriculum to avoid a superficial tourist approach to cultures, languages and minority groups. Only teachers who possess an intimate understanding of the point of these four pillars have the potential to protest and advocate for students that have been historically oppressed. Indeed, Bartolomé's argument resonates with Freire's, which works to persuade teachers to see through the 'dense of fog of ideology' and to act courageously to create a less biased and more democratic society (Bartolomé, 2003; 2004; 2008b; Freire, 1997).

REFERENCES

Bartolomé, L. (1998). *The misteaching of academic discourses. The politics of language in the classroom.* Boulder, CO: Westview Press.

Bartolomé, L. (2003). Democratizing Latino education: A perspective on elementary education. In V. I. Kloosterman (Ed.), *Latino students in American schools: Historical and contemporary views* (pp. 33–46). Westport, CT: Praeger.

Bartolomé, L. (2004). Critical pedagogy and teacher education: Radicalizing prospective teachers. *Teacher Education Quarterly, 31*(1), 97–122.

Bartolomé, L. (2006). The struggle for language rights: Naming and interrogating the colonial legacy of "English only". *Human Architecture: Journal of the Sociology of Self-Knowledge,* IV. Special Issue, 25–32.

Bartolomé, L. (2008a). Authentic cariño and respect in minority education: The political and ideological dimensions of love. *International Journal of Critical Pedagogy, 1*(1), 1–10.

Bartolomé, L. (2008b). *Ideologies in education: Unmasking the trap of teacher neutrality.* New York, NY: Peter Lang Pub Inc.

Bartolomé, L. (2010). Preparing to teach newcomer students: The significance of critical pedagogy and the study of ideology in teacher education. *Yearbook of the National Society for the Study of Education, 109*(2), 505–526.

Bartolomé, L. (2011). Literacy as comida: Learning to read with Mexican novellas. In M. de la Luz Reyes (Ed.), *Words were all we had. Becoming biliterate against the odds.* (pp. 49–59). New York: Teacher College Press.

Bartolomé, L., & Leistyna, P. (2006). Naming and interrogating our English only legacy. *Radical Teacher, 75,* 2–9.

Freire, P. (1997). *Mentoring the mentor: A critical dialogue with Paulo Freire.* New York: Peter Lang Pub Inc.

Macedo, D., & Bartolomé, L. (2001). *Dancing with bigotry: Beyond the politics of tolerance.* Basingstoke, UK: Palgrave MacMillan.

4. DEBORAH BRITZMAN

Critical Thinker, Researcher, Psychoanalyst

Deborah Britzman is one of the representatives of critical pedagogy who enters the classroom with courage to encounter its lively world where the complex interfacing of emotions, resistances, and perplexities unfold among the people that comprise a classroom setting. She keeps the door open and admits the presence of societal and cultural discourses, histories, myths, and a plethora of backgrounds which can be hidden and problematic but discoverable if one dares to see and examine them in a classroom environment. The focus of Britzman's work is to bring this almost neglected world to the stage and empower teachers to work within the realities of the classroom. Her familiarity with critical theory, the ideas of Frankfurt School and Feminist Theory is obvious. In examining the affective world of education, Britzman utilizes psychoanalysis in combination with queer theory to scratch off the surface of normalized and accepted schooling routines in order to explore what is occurring underneath those routines and other daily happenings.

BRIEF BACKGROUND

Britzman earned a Bachelor of Arts degree from the University of Massachusetts in 1972, and went on to teach high school English for seven years. It was during that time she was shocked to realize she had students who could not read, leaving her stumped on how to help them (Britzman, 2009a). Following a year of reading and reflection, Britzman enrolled at the University of Massachusetts-Amherst and earned a master's degree in reading and anthropology and later a Ph.D., completing an ethnographic study examining reading and literacy. Britzman began her career in higher education at Binghamton University, State University of New York in 1985, later moving on to accepting a position at York University in Toronto. It was during a fourth year in higher education that she began closely reading Freud and the important relevance of psychoanalysis. Discovering that all her areas of "experience" were becoming irrelevant because they were grounded solely in a United States setting, Britzman desired to employ a new area of study that was not so directed or dependent on her North American context (Britzman, 2009a). As a consequent, because of her deep interest in psychoanalysis, she decided to further her learning in that area. Currently, Britzman holds the honor of Distinguished Research Professor

James D. Kirylo (Ed.), A Critical Pedagogy of Resistance: 34 Pedagogues We Need to Know, 13–16.

at York University in Toronto and the designation of psychoanalyst in addition to her small private clinical practice.

CRITICAL THINKER, PSYCHOANALYSIS, AND EDUCATION

Exploring the emotional life and extending her search into the unconscious, Britzman brings an original vision to critical pedagogy. She is interested in the significant themes related to power, social justice, knowledge, feminist and queer theories, generating a critical point of view that focuses on the affective components of learning and on educational ethics. Britzman's reading of Paulo Freire's *Pedagogy of the Oppressed* had a significant impact on the way she thought about what it means to read, particularly with respect to Freire's notion of what it means to read the world (Britzman, 2009a). Freire's focus on the psychological, social, and economic aspects of reading and its relationship to the subject (reader) illuminated for Britzman the existential dynamic involved in the teaching and learning process. Reading became liberated from print and placed into the problem of interpretation which made literacy an interpretive art. Freire led Britzman to the works of Herbert Marcuse, Erich Fromm, Hannah Arendt, Herman Melville, and others, thus leading to a world of literature (learning) and a deep abiding interest to the status of the conflict in education (Britzman, 2009a).

Taking a psychoanalytical approach to education, Britzman explores how students live within a larger social context (school) that is often conflictive: communities, cultures, histories. She examines how students live within and with their individual selves as well; a psychological world that is just as conflictive as the external one. Dynamic and shifting, internal and external realities organize the self and the psyche (Britzman, 1998; 2003a; 2011). Psychoanalysis is a process for education to begin to notice the emotional world of students as a basis of understanding themselves and others. For example, Freud examined the unconscious, and within that realm he explored education as an experience that included our emotions and desires, themes that are rarely explored within the teaching and learning process. As a consequence of this lack, unexplored patterns of adaptation established in childhood educational experiences persist and remain as superficial filters well into adulthood.

Particularly for those entering teacher education programs, unexplored patterns of adaptation or infantile theories of learning ultimately limit one's ability to critically think and examine complexities inherent in education (Britzman, 2009a). Therefore, what naturally confronts that tension is to facilitate a critical environment that taps into our capacity to think, which is the experimental form of action. Moreover, an environment that fosters imagination is needed which is the grounds of our capability to read (learn), to take in the world, to construct what exists in the mind, and what comprises our desires. Reading frees the psyche, its grace, flexibility and imagination, and status of ideas. Without critical thought and imagination, the capability to bring things together, to feel, to love, to put meaning to the world would not exist (Britzman, 2009a).

Contrasting education with dreams, Britzman (2009b) argues that education leads one to the boarders of unconscious; it requires associations, interpretations and narratives capable of bringing to awareness for future constructions, things that are farthest from the mind. For Britzman, psychoanalysis is the approach needed to best understand the emotional meaning of education. This is realized in her written work where she—exploring psychoanalytic concepts as resistance, object relations and transference—gives a unique view to understand both dynamics of learning and phenomena that exists in a classroom (Britzman, 2006; 2007; 2011).

One of these phenomena is the resistance of one's personal development toward the quest for knowledge. This emerges from the need for security, whereby the act of learning is unfortunately linked to one's painful emotional experiences of helplessness, dependence and frustration (Britzman, 1998; 2006; 2007). Therefore, the concept of "difficult knowledge" means interference to one's personal security, leading toward internal conflict. That is, the passion to accept one's state in ignorance and to be simultaneously drawn to the internal invitation to know creates a contradictory situation (Britzman, 2003a). But without these resistances and desires, the pursuit toward knowledge remains untouched. Indeed, the dynamic interactions with individuals' internal and external realities and their conflicting substances are present in school. Therefore, it is all the more critical that the classroom setting is viewed as a space where pupils act on their ontological search and epistemological yearnings, establish their relationships with others, and discover the affective aspects of being (Britzman, 1998; 2003a; 2009b).

LEARNING AN IMPOSSIBLE PROFESSION

In her work *Practice makes Practice A Critical Study of Learning to Teach,* Britzman (2003b) frames her thought in critical theory and draws from ethnographic methods to study student teaching as a personal experience of learning and as the social reproduction of a practice. A teacher's struggles for constructing a teaching "voice" is not merely a personal phenomenon, but a struggle with authority, knowledge, and power to establish one's identity in the contradictory realities of school environments with its administrative and contextual strains and unwritten expectations.

According to Britzman (2003b), "The mass experience of public education has made teaching perhaps the most familiar profession" (pp. 26–27); consequently, teaching is overpopulated with cultural myths and unconscious rules. And through the experiences of Jamie Owl and Jack August, Britzman (2003b) illuminates how student teachers' (novices') efforts to think and act like teachers are undermined by social, cultural, historical, and political variables outside of their control. School institutions have traditions and practices that include language of power and authority, which tend to produce silence and exclusion. Even the curriculum might ignore emotions, sexuality, experiences, and knowledge of the very human being desirous of becoming a teacher (Britzman, 1998, 2003b). Thus, the existential tension of becoming a teacher means whether to conform to the given, normative practices of school, and thus joining the reproductive practices, or to begin to search out for the possible, more interactive world with diverse voices (Britzman, 1998; 2003b).

In searching, a teacher is never fully developed. Uncertainty and unevenness; the wandering mind, the responsibility and the affective relationships constitute the essence of education. A teacher works with human minds, and she or he guides newcomers to a world which she or he has not created. This is an ethical dilemma of education, to be dependent on and responsible for an unknown (Britzman, 2003b; 2006; 2007; 2009b; 2011). In the end, Bitzman's thought significantly contributes to our understanding of the complex world of teaching and learning.

REFERENCES

Britzman, D. (1998). *Lost subjects, contested objects. Toward a psychoanalytic inquiry of learning.* New York: State University Press.

Britzman, D. (2003a). *After-Education. Anna Freud, Melanie Klein, and psychoanalytic histories of learning.* New York: State University Press.

Britzman, D. (2003b). *Practice makes practice. A critical Study of learning to Teach* (2nd Ed). New York: State University Press

Britzman, D. (2006). *Novel education psychoanalytic studies of learning and not learning.* New York: Peter Lang

Britzman, D. (2007). Teacher education as uneven development: toward a psychology of uncertainty. *International Journal of Leadership in Education: Theory and Practice, 10*(1), 1–12.

Britzman, D. (2009a). Deborah Britzman on Freire and Psychoanalysis: Interview by Grüzel Aziz. [Video file]. Retrieved from http://vimeo.com/31747556

Britzman, D. (2009b). *The very thought of education. Psychoanalysis and the impossible professions.* New York: State University Press.

Britzman, D. (2011). *Freud and education.* New York: Routledge.

LYNDA ROBBIRDS DAUGHENBAUGH & EDWARD L. SHAW, JR.

5. JUDITH BUTLER

Philosophy of Resistance

INTRODUCTION

Judith Butler was born in Cleveland, Ohio in 1956 to Jewish parents of Russian and Hungarian heritage. Because her parents practiced different forms of Judaism, mother Orthodox and father Reformed, they decided to send Judith to Hebrew school to study and learn about religion for herself. She was considered a difficult child, always getting into trouble for not following teachers' instructions, being too loud, and too talkative. At age 14, her Hebrew teacher decided to punish her by requiring her to choose a philosopher to study so that she would not disrupt class with her questions and comments. Ironically, this "punishment" became the foundation for her life's work. As she immersed herself in reading and writing about philosophy, she became passionate about ideas, and eventually earned a PhD in Philosophy from Yale University in 1984. She identifies herself as a lesbian, an anti-Zionist Jew, and a critic of Israeli politics. Currently Butler is a Professor of Comparative Literature and Rhetoric at the University of California, Berkeley where she and her partner, well-known political scientist Wendy Brown, live together. Butler has one son.

AREAS OF INTEREST

Judith Butler is a post-structuralist philosopher whose main body of work includes numerous writings on feminist theory, queer theory, political philosophy, ethics, power, sexuality, and gender studies, greatly contributing to our understandings of sexual orientation, gender identity, and feminism in today's world. Butler's concept of "gender perfomativity", which she describes as the idea that each individual develops and performs gender in society as a result of social constructs and social norms, therefore positing the idea that gender is not something we are, but instead it is something that we do in our daily lives, is perhaps the most important and influential of all her theories. Butler also maintains that it is possible for an individual to choose his/her gender, but impossible in our society to choose no gender. To that end, the following provides an overview of Butler's thought as it relates to gender and sexuality, queer theory, feminism, ethics, and politics.

James D. Kirylo (Ed.), A Critical Pedagogy of Resistance: 34 Pedagogues We Need to Know, 17–20.
© *2013 Sense Publishers. All rights reserved.*

Gender and Sexuality

To understand Butler's theories about gender and sexuality, one must be open to questioning the belief that certain traditional behaviors assigned exclusively to either males or females is predetermined by nature (Butler, 1990). She asserts that notions of femininity and masculinity are acts or performances that have been imposed upon or ingrained into society by ideals of normative heterosexuality. In other words, many of our behaviors are determined for us within the realms of language, convention, and how our perceptions of reality are formed.

Butler further theorizes that identity creation is a process based on past acts which produces an illusion for society as a result of both understated and obvious pressures. When the normal is rejected, the defining limits are set for all who do not fall within these ranges, and they become part of what is considered by society as unnatural. Therefore, by highlighting the synthetic, restricted, and perfomative nature of gender identity, Butler further questions the universally accepted definitions of gender. This questioning is considered an affront to the status quo resulting in a forum in which she argues for the rights of particular groups of people, especially gays and lesbians, whom she views as being disregarded by those given power by mainstream society.

Queer Theory

Included in Butler's writings about feminism are thoughts and ideas that express the tradition of sexual freedom as an important aspect of feminism. She has avoided movements, writers, and groups who are highly regulative or repressive, particularly ones that attempt to establish norms for behaviors and sexuality that result in feminism being considered theory, and lesbianism the only possible practice because they disregard the sexual nature and desirous aspects of being a lesbian (Butler, 2004). However, she also respects the fact that women within the feminist movement who are bisexual or heterosexual also deserve respect. Butler explains that she became a lesbian out of desire for a particular person, and later became a participant in the politics of sexuality and gender identity as a result of this relationship.

Interestingly, when Butler (1990) discusses queer theory she is referring to a non conformist or dissident attitude rather than a synonym for homosexual. Universally, the queer theory movement refers to a philosophy and course of study intended to expand and explain the diversity of sexualities and cultural expressions of all people. The most important aspect of this point of view is looking at these issues from a stance of resistance to traditionally designated male and female roles across cultures and religions. Moreover, she notes that the movement which is seen by many to be radically democratic and sexually progressive is not always the case, and, in fact, is vulnerable to the same negative patterns as all other radical political movements. In the beginning it was thought to be a way of disregarding the importance of sexual identity, but politically it became much more. Butler views it as a way to illustrate the importance of people coming together to accomplish things, as well as the fact that people who can legitimately participate in this movement are not restricted from doing so because of their sexual orientation. The most critical ideas are those that are anti-institutional with respect to the notion of what it means to be "normal." Patterns of normalization as to what it means to be lesbian, gay or heterosexual and what defines sexual orientation as dictated by the limitation of labels are to be resisted. In the end, heterosexuals and bisexuals can join the queer movement because it is an argument against normalization and the limits it imposes on people.

Feminism

According to Butler (1990) the American feminist movement has been successful in securing reproductive rights, but the significant cultural differences within the movement obviously intersects with sexuality and race which naturally creates both weaknesses and strengths. Though causes like anti-pornography and sexual harassment law are very popular and are reported frequently by the mainstream media, it becomes in Butler's opinion, more of a movement for sexual purity than a movement for sexual freedom. Another problem is that feminism in America has traditionally been viewed as a white middle class movement, and this is especially true when looking at the leadership. Butler believes this problematic reality exists because of anti-feminism attitudes in minority communities, and their worries that supporting the feminist movement will diminish their commitment to the alliances they hope will improve conditions within their particular communities. But, more important is Butler's belief that feminism has not made a great impact in these areas because of its failure to make successful coalitions with anti-racial groups.

Ethics

With respect to ethics, Butler (2005) makes the point that we are limited by self-knowledge which is, in reality, never completely transparent to our own selves. Stated another way, we can become easily restricted by societal pressures, peer influences, and community norms. This limitation of self thusly marks us as incomplete, thereby causing us to be unable to be fully accountable for our actions. This lack of responsibility, for which one may be forgiven, is due to the fact that one could not help oneself. Not being able to control what one does in all cases becomes the predicament that causes Butler to argue for ethics based on the limitations of self-knowledge as the actual boundaries whereby responsibilities can be set. She further states that addressing ethics based on a completely transparent self, and being entirely accountable to oneself, does a great injustice to the self it tries to explain. Therefore, Butler sees ethics through a responsible self that knows it is limited in its self-knowledge, does not exceed its capacity to justify itself to others, and does not cross the boundaries that would change our genuine humanness. Butler posits that social and political critiques are at the core of ethical practice, and being able to accept one's limitations of self-knowledge allows one to be able to critically question the social world by which one is surrounded.

Politics

Butler is a self-described anti–Zionist because she disagrees with the hegemonic attitude of the Israeli government against the Palestinians who live in the Gaza Strip area. She believes that as a Jew she is obliged to speak about social injustice which means criticizing the state of Israel, but doing so may cause her to be deemed not a good enough Jew, or a self-hating Jew (Butler, 1997). That being said, she has a difficult time understanding how a people who have been oppressed for centuries are able to deny others that live within their borders basic human rights and social equality. She additionally argues that this attitude goes against Jewish teachings that life is precarious and should be protected. In this case Israeli separatism has become a reconstruction of the ghetto rather than emancipation for the Jewish state.

CONCLUSION

What makes the world livable, according to Butler, is not a question exclusively for philosophers, but for everyone. As we consider a philosophy of life, we need to not only consider the ethical nature of our point of view and the power relationships involved, but also to be mindful of what is important, what is of value, what is just, and what it is that makes us human.

REFERENCES

Butler, J. (2005). *Giving an account of oneself.* New York, NY: Routledge.

Butler, J. (2004). *Undoing gender.* New York, NY: Routledge.

Butler, J. (1997). *Excitable speech: Politics of the performance.* New York, NY: Routledge.

Butler, J. (1990). *Gender trouble: Feminism and the subversion of identity.* New York, NY: Routledge.

Judith Butler biography. Retrieved June 11, 2012. http://www.egs.edu/faculty/Judith-butler/biography Judith Butler biography. Retrieved June 11, 2012. http://www.facebook.com/note.php?note_id=148233231872879

Judith Butler: As a Jew, I was taught it was ethically imperative to speak up. Retrieved June 11, 2012. http://www.haaretz.com/news/judith-butler-as-a-jew-i-was-taught-it-was-ethically-imperative-to-speak-up-part-ii-1.266244

Felluga, D. Modules on butler: On gender and sex. *Introductory Guide to Critical Thinking.* (January 2011, last update).

Purdue U., Retrieved June 11, 2012. http://www.purdue.edu/guidetotheory/genderand sex/modules/butlergendersex.html

Queer theory. Retrieved June 11, 2012. http://www.sterneck.net/butler-queer/index.php

Queer theory. Retrieved June 11, 2012. http://www.lolapress.org/elec2/artenglish/butl_e.htm

Quotes by Judith Butler. Retrieved June 11, 2012. http://www.goodreads.com/author/show/5231

World English Dictionary. Retrieved June 11, 2012. http://dictionary.reference.com/browse/hegemonic

JANNA SIEGEL ROBERTSON

6. NOAM CHOMSKY

Father of Modern Linguistics

Noam Chomsky is a distinguished linguist, philosopher, cognitive psychologist, and political activist. A professor emeritus in linguistics at the Massachusetts Institute of Technology, Chomsky has written over 100 books and countless other publications. As a libertarian socialist with provocative political views and one that is guided by democratic ideals, a search for truth, and a quest for freedom, Chomsky's work principally focuses on concepts related to linguistics, cognition, education, and public policy (Hill, 2001).

LINGUISTICS AND COGNITION

Because his work has had a transformative effect in the field of linguistics, Chomsky is considered by many to be the "father of modern linguistics." Indeed, the "Chomskyan linguistics" movement is based on Chomsky's thought about the structures of language. He moves from describing existing languages to examining the commonalities of language and how they are acquired. In fact, his first contributions to critical pedagogy come from his early work in linguistics, rejecting behavioral learning theories when applied to language. He argues that there is an innate part of the human brain devoted to language and that it is a distinctive characteristic of being human (Chomsky, 2000). Chomsky makes the point that an inherent language acquisition device within all children provides for them limited in time frame during early childhood, in which they can acquire language at rapid rate. Children who do not learn language during this time will not have a true mastery of their native language as compared to other children who do learn communication during this crucial time period (Smith, 1999). Moreover, Chomsky asserts that a biological construct of language includes a universal grammar which is the basis for all languages. He explains that the differences in languages are not the structures, but the sounds that are associated with the words in the structures. Chomsky argues for what he characterizes as a generative grammar, which expands as people learn how to communicate (Chomsky, 1986; Smith, 1999). The best way to understand the human mind is through examining language, not that a mind could not exist without language, but it is our main indicator what is happening in the mind (Bovitch, Cullimore, Bramwell-Jones, Massas & Perun, 2011; Smith, 1999).

James D. Kirylo (Ed.), A Critical Pedagogy of Resistance: 34 Pedagogues We Need to Know, 21–24.
© 2013 Sense Publishers. All rights reserved.

According to Chomsky, learning is innate, and occurs through a process of exploration and discovery. However, for discovery to occur a frame of reference must necessarily be in place. For example, the Internet provides a wealth of information, but one needs a clear direction or framework for the inquiry to be fruitful — merely reading a "random set of factoids" can be harmful, since one is not able to contextually evaluate the information. However, if there is a theoretical basis or clear point of view for the inquiry, learning is more readily going to take place since there is prior knowledge to assist the learner to critically evaluate the new information. To more concretely make the point, a Nobel Prize recipient is not necessarily awarded to one who simply reads the most; rather, recipients are those who are theoretically and conceptually rooted and know what to look for and what is worthy of close examination (Chomsky, 2012a).

VIEWS ON EDUCATION: AN OVERVIEW

Chomsky maintains that everyone should be given the opportunity to be educated since inherently we all possess the desire to be challenged and to expand our possibilities (Bovitch et. al., 2011). Attending school, however, is not the same as receiving an education. That is, schools can either be places that teach students how to learn or they can be places where they are indoctrinated. Chomsky argues that historically the purpose of mass education is to systematically create and control a people who become compliant and submissive members of society, thusly preventing the masses to perceive themselves as free and empowered to dare and question (Chomsky in an interview by Leistyna & Sherblom, 1995).

Chomsky (1999) suggests that there seems to be a relationship where the more educators profess their democratic spaces, the less this seems to be the concrete reality. He also makes clear that the purpose of education is to enable students to become critical thinkers and good human beings, rejecting the notion that the primary purpose of education is economic growth and immediate financial success for students. While teaching can be a "common sense" affair, Chomsky notably advises teachers to meaningfully tap into student interest and their natural curiosities where learning is relevant and intrinsic, which can evolve through a process of exploration, discovery, and creativity. This act of discovery naturally will promote innovations and economic growth, not as a primary goal, but as a logical extension or outcome of education (Chomsky, 2012a).

Providing an example of what a more democratic and critical thinking model looks like, Chomsky describes the Massachusetts Institute of Technology (MIT) as a place where discovery is freely encouraged due to the entire university's scientific focus. While the sciences survive on the basis of creativity and to challenge existing theories and constructs, non-scientific disciplines and their existing frameworks are used to exert control over the academics (Hill, 2001). Chomsky tellingly put it this way some years ago when he stated, "You can lie or distort the story of the French

Revolution as long as you like and nothing will happen. Propose a false theory in chemistry, and it'll be refuted tomorrow" (Barsky, 1997, p. 11).

Assessment

Chomsky has described the "factory model of schools" in which students are subjected to a mandated curriculum, with an emphasis on skill and drill in order to prepare for multiple choice exams (Bovitch et al., 2011). He obviously realizes the relevance and purpose of assessment, but urges caution regarding the overdependence on testing as a source of student information. In other words, while one individual may achieve well on a test, he/she may nevertheless possess very little deep understanding of the topic compared to another individual who may have innovative ideas yet not do well on standardized type tests. In the end, Chomsky (2012a) argues that tests not only have limitations, but they can also be used as obstacles to foster authentic learning, explorations, and discovery.

Privatization

Chomsky is wary of schools not under public control, and believes that corporations are "private tyrannies." Believing that the corporate takeover of education has been in the works for years, Chomsky claims that the route to private control of any public institution is to underfund it or create a plan that will not work. Once the institution is discredited, then there is a clamor for it to be privatized in order to save it (Hill, 2001). However, despite the growing trend of privatization and corporate-run schools, Chomsky does not believe that schools are necessarily doomed, arguing that intellectuals, including practitioners, can challenge the current trends and succeed. He is optimistic that society is better off now than ever and that despite his criticisms of America, we are the "freest civilization in the world" (Chomsky in an interview with Hill, 2001). Because of our democracy, we can stand up and make changes with only marginal social costs as compared to most other countries or other periods of history (Hill, 2001).

Politics

Chomsky has been an outspoken critic of the United States and Israel for most of his career (Barsky, 1997). As a critical pedagogue who believes that freedom is essential for progress, it is not surprising that Chomsky is quick to point out when he notices policies and practices that limit democracy. When it comes to the major political parties in the U.S, he is disparaging of both the Republicans and Democrats, arguing that the former is a puppet for financial institutions and corporations, and the latter is ideologically driven by a Republican mindset and also caters to corporate greed. Indeed, the U.S government has been corrupted by corporate America wherein most of the policies and laws decidedly benefit the wealthy at the expense of the general populace, ultimately limiting the freedom for all Americans (Chomsky, 2012b & 2012c).

Chomsky has a long history of commenting on American foreign policy, succinctly asserting that American interests are imperialistic in the attempt of promoting policies that further their influence in the world. These include supporting Israel which has a sophisticated military defense capability, rather than their Arab counterparts who are seemingly under better control when they are under dictator regimes supported by the U.S. In the final analysis, Chomsky has consistently been outspoken of U.S. policy when it selfishly looks out for their economic interests at the expense of exploitive practices that may inhibit or limit democracy and freedom in other countries around the world (Chomsky, 2012b, 2012c).

CONCLUSION

Critical pedagogy is ultimately an endeavor to create a more just, ethical, and free society. And as a critical pedagogue, Chomsky's views on linguistics, cognition, education, and politics all possess a common theme that underscores that authentic learning and human progress only occurs when an individual is at liberty to inquire, question, and challenge the status quo. Any interference that subverts that process is unacceptable.

REFERENCES

Barsky, R. (1997). *Noam Chomsky: A life of dissent*. MIT Press. Retrieved online September 15, 2012 from http://cognet.mit.edu/library/books/chomsky/chomsky/

Bovitch, S., Cullimore, Z., Bramwell-Jones, T., Massas, E., & Perun, D. (2011). The educational theory of noam chomsky. *New foundations*. Retrieved June 28, 2012 from http://www.newfoundations.com/GALLERY/Chomsky.html

Chomsky, N. (2012a). The purpose of education. *Learning without frontiers*. January 25, 2012. Retrieved June 28, 2012 from http://blip.tv/learning-without-frontiers/noam-chomsky-the-purpose-of-education-5925460

Chomsky, N. (2012b). *"Losing" the world: American decline in perspective, Part 1"* Retrieved from Tomdispatch.com on September 15, 2012.

Chomsky, N. (2012c). *"The imperial way: American decline in perspective, Part 2"* Retrieved from Tomdispatch.com on September 15, 2012.

Chomsky, N. (2000). Linguistics and brain science. In A. Marantz, Y. Miyashita & W. O'Neil (Eds.), *Image, language and brain*. Cambridge, MA: MIT Press.

Chomsky, N. (1999). *Chomsky on miseducation*. London, UK: Oxford.

Chomsky, N. (1986). *Knowledge of language: Its nature, origin, and use*. New York: Praeger.

Hill, P. (2001). Public education and moral monsters: A conversation with Noam Chomsky. *Our schools/our selves*. Ottawa, Canada: CCPA.

Leistyna, P., & Sherblom, S. (1995). A dialogue with Noam Chomsky: On violence and youth. *Harvard Educational Review, 65*(2), 127–44.

Smith, N. (1999). *Chomsky ideas and ideals*. Cambridge, UK: Cambridge.

LINDA PICKETT

7. ANTONIA DARDER

A Passionate, Courageous, and Committed Critical Pedagogue

Passion, courage and commitment immediately come to mind when I think of Antonia Darder. Her passion for social justice and equality fuels her fearless critique of power, politics and education, while her enduring commitment sustains her work through difficult and strident political times. Framed in the powerful virtue of hope, the work of Darder is simultaneously complex and simple. That is, the simplicity of her unwavering belief in the inherent dignity and worth of all human beings lays a stalwart foundation for her complex and ever-evolving theories. As it is not possible to adequately discuss the range of Darder's contributions to the field of critical pedagogy within the confines of this chapter, I chiefly focus upon the integrity of her work as a critical theorist who truly walks the talk of reflection, reinvention and transformation.

BRIEF BACKGROUND

Born in Puerto Rico, Antonia Darder is an extraordinary human being who came to the United States as a young child. Raised in East Los Angeles by a single mother, Darder describes living the first 26 years of her life in poverty (The Freire Project, 2012). Her journey to becoming an internationally known critical theorist is unique and rich with experiences that inform her work. Herself a single mother of three daughters, Darder defied the odds and first studied at a community college and went on to become a pediatric nurse, and later a psychotherapist.

Although she was already a seasoned community activist, her study of the relationships that shape power, politics and education began when she attended a conference on the work of Paulo Freire. There, she encountered a theoretical foundation that aligned with and expanded on her lifelong interests in culture, empowerment, and equality. Upon that foundation, she engaged in critical explorations of privilege, oppression, power and politics in education. As a working-class Latina, Darder brought fresh and vital perspectives to the field of critical pedagogy. With her scholarship, lived experience and critical reflections, she continues to speak with a voice of authenticity that brings complex theoretical frameworks to life. When Darder calls for education that is transformative and liberating, she speaks with authority, as one who is informed by her own life experience as well as by scholarship. Indeed, Freire, who was her mentor, colleague and friend, profoundly influenced Darder.

James D. Kirylo (Ed.), A Critical Pedagogy of Resistance: 34 Pedagogues We Need to Know, 25–28.

And while her work clearly reflects that influence, she moves beyond his theories, exhibiting Freire's exhortation to all critical pedagogues that "...we should reinvent your [Freire's] ideas, build on them, transform them, understand them as historical contributions of a particular moment in time..." (Darder, 1998, p. 256).

Critical Ideas

Her influential text *Culture and Power in the Classroom: A Critical Foundation for Bicultural Education* (1991) examines and courageously proclaims relationships regarding power, politics and education that perpetuate social privilege and oppression, while also contributing essential insights into the realities of living and learning as a bicultural student. These insights provide a foundation for educators to examine their own beliefs, critique current practices, and develop practices that value and support students. *Culture and Power in the Classroom* also introduces educators to the notion of praxis as the key to emancipatory education. By explaining and promoting the idea that theory and practice go hand in hand, she calls upon teachers to understand themselves, their students and their own practice as situated within the workings of a social context characterized by hegemony, ideology, resistance and cultural invasion.

The new edition, *Culture and Power in the Classroom: Educational Foundations for the Schooling of Bicultural Students* (2012), is timely as educators and students struggle in a political climate characterized by racism, denial of inequalities, and demands for "excellence" as demonstrated through ever more testing. Those demands have resulted in an increasingly narrow and biased curriculum while ignoring the needs, desires and realities of students, families, and teachers as well as the science of learning. Darder demonstrates the fallacy of this approach by identifying the functions of racism and classism in schooling that perpetuate privilege and oppression as she explains the devastating consequences for bicultural students. As her robust critiques address both liberal and conservative ideologies, her stance is human-centered in urging for a fundamental change in how education is defined. That is, she calls for radical educational practice that responds to the needs, dreams and aspirations of *all* students, rather than preparing hierarchies of workers to bolster a capitalist economy.

Darder challenges teachers to become politically aware of inequitable conditions and policies that define schooling, while simultaneously examining their own ideologies and pedagogical purposes. Yet, she stresses that knowing is not enough and calls for action to protect students from harmful practices and create safe, supportive spaces for learning. To do so, she maintains that teachers must be willing to learn from and about students as individuals and as cultural beings. At the same time, teachers need to learn to understand the challenges faced by students and families who must juggle different and inequitable cultural worlds. To that end, Darder inspires educators to examine and confront the conditions that promote mounting xenophobia and violence in current times and to act in ways that empower students to change present conditions, thereby creating history.

In a speech giving tribute to the life and work of Paulo Freire, Darder (1998) addresses tensions within the field of critical pedagogy. In particular, she discusses the conflict between Freire's focus on class distinctions and class conflict as primary sources of oppression, and the views held by scholars of color who identify racism as an equally important cause of division and oppressive social hierarchy. While Freire acknowledged racism, he believed that sexism and racism are imbedded within the class factor of the social hierarchy. He emphasized that division and sectarianism bolster the aims of capitalism and urged solidarity of oppressed groups in the human struggle for liberation. Scholars of color maintained that such solidarity could not be achieved unless racism itself was addressed as a form of oppression.

Darder's discussion of those tensions and her subsequent publication of *Shattering the "Race" Lens: Toward a Critical Theory of Racism* (Darder & Torres, 2003) demonstrate the dynamic and evolving nature of critical theory. Within a complex and fascinating argument, Darder and Torres posit that the very idea of race is a social construction that functions to create division and conflict among groups of people whose very division subjects them to exploitation and domination in capitalist economies. Thus, the notion of race, defined by difference and conflicting interests creates racism. Likewise, groups of people are racialized, not by absolute criteria for defining collective groups, but according to economic imperatives. Indeed, racist ideology does divide oppressed groups, making exploitation of oppressed groups possible as it undermines solidarity. While this emerging theory validates Freire's concern that solidarity in the social justice movement is blocked by identity politics, it goes beyond merely identifying the problem to demonstrating that although notions of race are subjective constructs, those individual and collective identities are so deeply entrenched in worldviews, that they cannot be simply ignored. Therefore, the purposes and processes of racialization must be deconstructed and understood in order to challenge unexamined beliefs about race as legitimate criteria for categories to define human beings. As it dismantles the legitimacy of racist ideologies, a critical theory of racism promises to contribute a framework for considering sociopolitical theory and practice through a democratic lens free of distortions and distractions of false divisions.

CONCLUSION

This brief look at the work of Antonia Darder only touches the surface of her contributions to critical pedagogy, yet it does illustrate the integrity with which she lives and works in relation to her theoretical view of education as a humanizing experience. It is telling that Darder (2012) credits her students for having "taught me the most about the communal nature of knowledge and the emancipator power of teaching and learning together with grace" (pp. xvi). The latter clearly reflects the nature of a teacher/learner engaged in the dialogical practice of liberatory education. While her scholarship is impressive with numerous publications and scholarly lectures, Darder further expresses herself through poetry and works of art that make her ideas accessible in broad venues. Even as she is a highly respected scholar, Darder is equally an activist who continues to work in solidarity with communities of students, educators, immigrants and workers through projects including the California Consortium of Critical Educators, radio programs and community publications focused on social transformation. Without a doubt, Darder's life and work embody the ideal of praxis and the very premises of the concept of democratic education to which she has so profoundly shaped.

REFERENCES

Darder, A. (1991). *Culture and power in the classroom: A critical foundation for bicultural education.* New York, NY: Bergin-Garvey.

Darder, A. (1998). Epilogue: A letter to him who dared to teach. In A. Darder *Reinventing Paulo Freire* (pp. 255–257). Cambridge, MA: Westview.

Darder, A. (1998). *Teaching as an act of love: In memory of Paulo Freire.* Paper presented at the American Educational Research Association, San Diego, CA. Retrieved from ERIC database. (ED426154)

Darder, A. (2012). *Culture and power in the classroom: Educational foundations for the schooling of bicultural students.* Boulder, CO: Paradigm.

Darder, A., & Torres, R. D. (2003). Shattering the "race" lens: Toward a critical theory of racism. In A. Darder, M. Baltodano, & R. D. Torres (Eds.), *The critical pedagogy reader* (pp. 245–261). New York, NY: Routledge.

The Freire Project (2012). *Antonia Darder.* Retrieved from http://www.freireproject.org/content/antonia-darder

ELIZABETH WADLINGTON

8. JOHN DEWEY

Pragmatist, Philosopher, and Advocate of Progressive Education

INTRODUCTION

Born in Burlington, Vermont in 1859, John Dewey is internationally recognized for his pragmatic philosophy and progressive education theory. Dewey received his Ph.D. from Johns Hopkins in 1884, and then went on to teach at the University of Michigan and the University of Minnesota. He later moved to the University of Chicago where he became chairman of the department of philosophy, psychology and pedagogy. It was at the University of Chicago where he founded his famed Lab School in which he carefully examined his pedagogical ideas in practice. He was elected president of the American Psychological Association in 1899 and the American Philosophical Association in 1905. That same year he began teaching at Colombia University where he stayed until his retirement in 1929, but continued serving as professor emeritus. While at Colombia, he traveled extensively expressing his ideas on philosophy, social and political theory, and education (Campbell, 1995; Hickman and Alexander, 1998). His own world was affected by Darwin's theory of evolution, rapid urbanization of society, and massive immigration to the United States. Thus, he questioned how education in such a democracy should be understood and practiced, advocating that theory, philosophy, and practical experiences should be interrelated (Dewey, 1915; Dewey, 1938). As a result, he wrote prolifically about education and other areas such as democracy, logic, art, nature, politics, religion, and ethics. He died at the age of ninety-two in 1952 (Campbell, 1995; Hickman and Alexander, 1998).

EDUCATION AND SOCIETY

Viewing individuals as adaptable biological and social organisms, Dewey (1897) asserted that education consists of a social and a psychological process. The psychological process, or the powers and activities of the child, should be the foundation of education; otherwise, education is arbitrary. But children are also social individuals with society being an organic union of these social beings. As a result, one cannot eliminate the social factor from the child or the individual factor from society.

James D. Kirylo (Ed.), A Critical Pedagogy of Resistance: 34 Pedagogues We Need to Know, 29–32.
© *2013 Sense Publishers. All rights reserved.*

Dewey (1916) believed that education is a continuous reconstruction of experience neither just to prepare for the future nor to reiterate the past. Indeed education is life itself. Education's purpose is to realize one's own potential and use one's skills for the good of society rather than learn a predetermined skill set. It begins when one is born and continues throughout life (Dewey, 1897). What the wisest parents want for their offspring should be what society wants for all children; hence, education should be universal (Dewey, 1915). Therefore, education is a process by which all individuals can participate in the social consciousness of the human race. As they share in social consciousness, they naturally adjust their own activities resulting in social reform and progress (Dewey, 1897).

According to Dewey (1915) democratic habits should begin early, and the school should be viewed as an extension of society. That is, schools should be connected to their surroundings (e.g., home, nature, business, museums, universities, and professional schools), which should necessarily lead students to cooperate and even collaborate with others in the community to actively pursue joint interests in fostering a democratic way of living. Seeing connections with the realities of life, students can take their own unique understandings and skills home to their families and put them to work focusing on real problems in the larger society. In sum, education should guide people to use their diverse gifts and talents for productive, interactive lives in order to promote a progressive society that values freedom, individualism, and the overall betterment of society (Dewey, 1916; 1915).

THE SCHOOL AND LEARNING

Dewey (1897) espoused that school, being a social institution and a simplified form of community life, should gradually grow out of the child's home life. In order to naturally lead the student to greater knowledge and skills, the school environment should nurture children based upon the child's four innate inclinations: a) the social instinct or communicating with others; b) the constructive impulse or desire to make things; c) the investigative instinct or the wish to explore/find out; and d) the expressive instinct or the desire for artistic expression (Dewey, 1902; Dewey, 1915). Because real life incorporates all subject areas, education's subject matter should come from the social life of the child integrating all traditional subjects (e.g., science, history, geography). The value of any subject depends upon its contribution to immediate significance of experience, and progress in school should not be measured by a sequence of subject matter but rather growth (Dewey, 1897; Dewey, 1916).

However, Dewey (1902) cautioned that over reliance on the child as the center of the curriculum is harmful. Consequently, the teacher should serve as a guide of learning utilizing subject matter as it relates to the child's developing interests and experiences. Moreover, the teacher's task is to prepare the environment for the child to learn through active engagement with and reflection upon continuous, interactive experiences. Learning should be a collaborative process between students and faculty recognizing that learners not only adapt to their environment but also actively change it (Dewey, 1897; Dewey, 1902).

Dewey advocated that learning how to think or problem solve should be the focus of education. Learning must be based upon the learner's questions, and investigation using the scientific method is the best way for intelligence to be cultivated (Dewey, 1903; Dewey, 1938). Authentic learning occurs when a real problem arises from first-hand experiences; children think about and suggest solutions; then they conduct active experimental testing of their ideas. In other words, reflective thinking is critical to learning, which not only supports an experiential approach to education, but also stimulates the desire to learn (Dewey, 1916; 1933; 1938).

In addition to the above, Dewey theorized about other aspects of learning as well. He viewed child's play as a worthwhile endeavor that would grow into more sophisticated activity and gradually pass into meaningful work. Knowing that children have an active, rich imaginary world, schools should train the child's power of imagery for optimal progress (Dewey, 1897; Dewey, 1902; Dewey, 1915; 1916). Dewey also valued manual or vocational training to help children become responsible, develop good habits, and realize the relationships between school and life (Dewey, 1903; Dewey, 1915). Fine arts and applied arts should be unified and brought into the everyday life of the learner allowing the viewer of art to participate in the creative experience with the artist (Dewey, 1934). He asserted that the best moral training comes through entering into appropriate social relationships to cooperate with others in work and thought (Dewey, 1897). Dewey advocated that all progress depends upon the teacher; teachers need to be empowered to have an educational voice; and every member of the school community must share educational power. What to teach and how to teach should be integrated into teacher education, and university laboratory schools should be labs for applied psychology (Dewey, 1903; 1915).

INFLUENCE TODAY

Dewey's concept of education as a moral and social force is relevant to contemporary society (Hickman, 2009). His idea of universal education to prepare citizens of a democracy is still recognized as critical for a democratic society to achieve its full potential (Hytten, 2009; false Rosenthal, 1993). Educators who advocate developmentally-appropriate, process-oriented, hands-on learning emphasizing children's interests and needs adhere to ideals that Dewey pioneered. Concepts such as the teacher as facilitator, experiential learning, use of the scientific method, and connecting schools to the larger community are held up as worthy goals for today (Ornstein, Levine, Gutek, and Vocke, 2010; Tanner, 1997). Many believe that today's leaders would do well to reconsider Dewey's beliefs regarding the role of university laboratory schools, teacher preparation programs, authentic educational assessment, and empowerment of teachers (Null, 2003; Tanner, 1997). In short, John Dewey ranks as one of the greatest educational thinkers of all times. His vision of education has been influential in the past, is relevant to the present, and may be drawn upon to face the challenges of the future.

REFERENCES

Campbell, J. (1995). *Understanding John Dewey: Nature and cooperative intelligence*. Chicago, IL: Open Court.

Dewey, J. (1897). My pedagogic creed. *The School Journal, 54*(3), 77–80.

Dewey, J. (1902). *The child and curriculum*. Chicago, IL: University of Chicago Press.

Dewey, J. (1903). Democracy in education. *The Elementary School Teacher, 4*(4),193–204.

Dewey, J. (1915). *The school and society*. Chicago, IL: University of Chicago Press.

Dewey, J. (1916). *Democracy and education: An introduction to the philosophy of education*. New York, NY: Macmillan.

Dewey, J. (1933). *How we think: Analysis of reflective thinking*. In Hickman, L. and Alexander, T.'s (Eds.), *The essential Dewey* (Vol. 2). (1998), Indianapolis, IN: Indiana University Press.

Dewey, J. (1934). *Art as experience*. New York, NY: Minton, Bach & Company.

Dewey, J. (1938). *Experience and education*. New York, NY: Macmillan.

Hickman., L. (2009). John Dewey at 150: Continuing relevance for a global milieu. *Educational Theory, 59*(4), 375–378.

Hickman, L. and Alexander, T. (Eds.) (1998). *The essential Dewey* (Vol. 2). Indianapolis, IN: Indiana University Press.

Hytten, K. (2009). Deweyan democracy in a globalized world. *Educational Theory, 59*(4), 395–408.

Null, J. (2003). John Dewey's child and the curriculum 100 years later. *American Educational History Journal, 30*, 59–68

Ornstein, A., Levine, D., Gutek, G., & Vocke, D. (2010). Foundations of education. Belmont, CA: Wadsworth.

Rosenthal, S. (1993). Democracy and education: A Deweyan approach. *Educational Theory, 43*(4), 377–390.

Tanner, L. (1997). *Dewey's laboratory school: Lessons for today*. New York, NY: Teachers College Press.

JOHN C. FISCHETTI

9. W.E.B. DU BOIS

The Roots of Critical Race Theory

Through his teaching, writing, speaking and leadership, William Edward Burghardt 'W. E. B.' Du Bois is one of the grandparents of multicultural education, later developed by James Banks, and critical race theory, advanced by Gloria Ladson-Billings (among others), into a discipline seeking equity and social justice for those "left behind" by slavery, disenfranchisement and ongoing race, class and gender divisions. A figurative, self-made pedagogue, Du Bois was born in 1868, three years after the end of the Civil War, was a witness to reconstruction, Jim Crow, World War I, the Great Depression, World War II, the rise of communism, Brown v. Board, the Cold War and the roots of the Civil Rights movement. He died in1963, the year President Kennedy was assassinated, and one year before the Voting Rights Act was passed. Du Bois' life shaped nearly a century of reactive and proactive responses to the elimination of slavery and injustice.

PERSONAL JOURNEY

Born in Massachusetts to an African American mother and a father of French-American and Haitian descent, the roots of Du Bois' social views were shaped by an accepting pluralistic culture in western Massachusetts at the time (W. E. B. Du Bois, 2012). Primarily raised by his mother, Du Bois attended public schools where there was an acceptance of difference. Consequently, the education he received allowed him to develop writing and verbal skills that empowered him to seek college admission. His local church provided the funds to send him to Fisk University in Nashville, an historically Black college (Buckley, K. (n.d.). During his college years, Du Bois kindled his African American heritage and continued refining his social and political views. Living in the Jim Crow south, he witnessed first-hand overt, blatant racism, which fueled his intellectual desire to study the roots of difference through the lenses of sociology, history and economics. After graduation from Fisk, Du Bois entered Harvard University; however, the administration there did not accept his academic degree from Fisk, forcing him to "repeat college" at his own expense. Under the tutelage of philosopher William James, Du Bois completed his second degree in three years, which steered him to enter graduate school at Harvard with support from a scholarship. While conducting his graduate work, he traveled abroad, including studying in Berlin where he was influenced by emerging German views

James D. Kirylo (Ed.), A Critical Pedagogy of Resistance: 34 Pedagogues We Need to Know, 33–36.
© *2013 Sense Publishers. All rights reserved.*

of science and European sociologists' scholarship, all of which helped him refine his understanding of power and race. (Buckley, K. n.d.). In 1895, with a dissertation title, *The Suppression of the African Slave Trade to the United States of America, 1638–1870*, Du Bois was the first student of African American descent to earn a Ph.D. from Harvard (NAACP.org, 2012).

PROFESSIONAL JOURNEY

Du Bois' desire to understand his own mixed ethnic heritage, and the contrasting experiences of his youth, led him to seek further intellectual study of the conditions of people of color as a professor in the academy, first in Ohio at Wilberforce University and then at the University of Pennsylvania. In his work studying Philadelphia neighborhoods, Du Bois published the first study of a Negro neighborhood, *The Philadelphia Negro* (1899). Du Bois relocated again to Atlanta University, returning to the south where he had first-hand experience of the failure of White society to embrace full equality of former slaves. He began to write extensively about the Negro experience and the importance of not accepting White society's master/former slave mentality (W. E. B. Du Bois, 2012). Du Bois particularly pushed back at Booker T. Washington, one of the most preeminent scholars and leaders of the African American community in the south. In Du Bois' view, Washington had capitulated to the White establishment in voting rights, employment issues and in maintaining segregation and White dominance for the promise of educational and economic opportunities. Du Bois staunchly urged Blacks not to be passive. His critique of Washington's *Up From Slavery* is a treatise on social change theory (Washington, 1901). Du Bois later published *The Souls of Black Folk* (1903), a manifesto revealing that the master will never relinquish his hold on the oppressed. In *Souls* Du Bois rhetorically raised the stature of Black culture to that equal to White culture—and challenged the deficit model born from slavery and perpetuated 300 years later by habit, custom, prejudice and law (Johnson & Watson, 2004, Kincheloe, 2008). He straightforwardly proposed that race research from a dominant perspective perpetuated the assumption that descendants of slaves were "problems" to be studied. Du Bois' work continued with others in Niagara Falls, New York in 1906 with the issuance of the Niagara Movement, a doctrine against submissiveness of Blacks to Whites (Lewis, 1995). Following a period of violence against Blacks supported by White leaders across the country, Du Bois urged Blacks to withdraw their support from the Republican Party, the party of Lincoln and emancipation (The Circle Association, 2012).

As a result of the increased violence and continued Jim Crow conditions, Du Bois assisted in the creation in 1909 of the National Association for the Advancement of Colored People (NAACP), serving as lead editor of *The Crisis*, the magazine of the organization. Using his role with the NAACP, Du Bois encouraged and helped establish the training of Black military officers in World War I (Johnson, 2000, NAACP.org, 2012). The failure of the military establishment to fully integrate Blacks, and the multiple situations in which blatant racist acts continued during the war, convinced Du Bois that a Pan-African movement was a logical resolution to the racial strife Blacks faced (Rabuka, 2003, Buckley, n.d.). After major philosophical differences, Du Bois distanced himself from Pan-African movement leader, Marcus Garvey, who advocated that African Americans should help lead an African resurgence on the mother continent (Rucker, 2002).

In his later years, Du Bois was an anti-war and anti-nuclear weapons advocate, studied socialism and communism across the world and strongly protested American military, political and economic imperialism. During Joseph McCarthy's trials against those who were purported to be anti-American, Du Bois was tried for acting as an agent of an enemy state in his pronouncements (NAACP.org, 2012). The NAACP gave him only lukewarm support during his trial. While not convicted, Du Bois became disenfranchised, his passport taken by the government for eight years. After running for senator from New York and continuing to write primarily on anti-war positions, Du Bois sought refuge through his travels to Africa (NAACP.org, 2012). He was invited to Ghana to develop an encyclopedia of Diaspora, the story of the movement of African people away from the continent. After the U.S. denied his passport renewal, Du Bois became a citizen of Ghana where he died in 1963 at the age of 95 (NAACP.org, 2012, Spartacus Educational, 2012).

LEGACY

The concept of race is a social construct not a biological reality. Du Bois' personal journey to understand his multicultural heritage in a Black and White world led him to use the intellectual pulpit to influence American society. His advocacy became a combination of multicultural education, critical pedagogy, critical race theory, change theory and anti-race theory. By critiquing the dominant philosophy that had created slavery as a sanctioned institution in the first place, and which continued to perpetuate the racial divide, Du Bois reclaimed intellectual prowess for people of color in the United States. While his inner struggle to sort out his mulatto roots evolved over his lifetime, Du Bois remained committed to his refusal to accept that the original roots of slavery were justified. He strongly argued that the condition of slavery had in no way lessened the dignity or intellectual potential of former slaves. His contributions as a pedagogue to critical race theory are in establishing the pretense that White domination was itself the problem, not the overcoming of inequities by a people of similar continental ancestry who had been persistently, deliberately and pervasively denied basic human rights in a democracy created by individuals who swore to protect those very rights.

REFERENCES

Buckley, K. (n.d.) *Du Bois: A concise biography*. Retrieved from http://www.library.umass.edu/spcoll/dubois/?page_id=861

The Circle Association. (2012). *The African American history of western New York*. Retrieved from http://www.math.buffalo.edu/~sww/0history/hwny-niagara-movement.html

Du Bois, W. E. B. (1899). *The Philadelphia Negro: A social study*. Philadelphia: University of Pennsylvania Press.

Du Bois, W. E. B. (1903). *The souls of Black folks*. Chicago: McClurg.

Du Bois, W. E. B. (1984). Dusk of dawn: An essay toward an autobiography of a race *concept*. New Brunswick, NJ and London: Transaction Books.

Du Bois, W. E. B. (1996). Darkwater: Voices from within the veil. The Oxford W.E.B. *Du Bois reader*. Edited by Eric J. Sundquist. New York and Oxford: Oxford University Press.

W.E.B. Du Bois. (2012). *Biography.com*. Retrieved from http://www.biography.com/people/web-du-bois-9279924

Johnson, D. (2000). W.E.B. Du Bois, Thomas Jesse Jones and the struggle for social education, 1900–1930. The *Journal of Negro History*, *85*(3), 71–95. Retrieved from http://www.jstor.org/stable/2649057

Johnson, D. & Watson, E. (2004). The W. E. B. Du Bois and Booker T. Washington debate: Effects upon African American roles in engineering and engineering technology. *The Journal of Technology Studies*, *30*(4), 65–70.

Kincheloe, J. L. (2008). *Critical pedagogy*. New York, NY: Peter Lang Publishing.

Lewis, D. L. (Ed.). (1995). *W.E.B. Du Bois, A reader*. New York: Henry Holt and Company.

NAACP.org. (2012). *NAACP history: W. E. B. Du Bois*. Retrieved from http://www.naacp.org/pages/naacp-history-w.e.b.-dubois

Rabuka, R. (2003). W.E.B. Du Bois' evolving Africana philosophy of education. *Journal of Black Studies*, *33*(4), 400–402.

Rucker, W. (2002). "'A Negro nation within the nation': W.E.B. DuBois and the creation of a revolutionary Pan-Africanist tradition, 1903–1947." *Black Scholar*, *22*(3/4), 37–47.

Spartacus Educational. (2012). William Du Bois. Retrieved from http://www.spartacus.schoolnet.co.uk/USAdubois.htm#source

Washington, B. T. (1901). *Up from slavery*. New York: Doubleday, Page & Company.

KRIS SLOAN

10. MICHAEL ERIC DYSON

A Man of God, Intellectual, Provocateur

To offer a spirited defense of justice, challenge reductive notions of race and class in America, render a critical reading of Nas's *Illmatic,* Michael Eric Dyson preaches, teaches, writes, debates, and sometimes even raps. Dyson is an ordained Baptist minister, a distinguished professor, a prolific researcher and writer, a "hip-hop intellectual," the host of a syndicated radio show, and a frequent contributor on cable news shows. He has been named one the most inspiring and one of the most influential Black Americans. In short, Michael Eric Dyson is one of our nation's foremost public intellectuals and his works on race, class, gender, sexual identity, and hip-hop offer educators many valuable and important insights.

EARLY BACKGROUND

A self-described "ghetto kid" from the west side of Detroit who showed early academic promise, Dyson endured hardships common to many young men of color in our inner cities. His life took a dramatic turn when an influential Detroit preacher took notice of the eleven-year old Dyson, winning him a scholarship to Cranbrook, a private, almost exclusively White boarding school. Dyson's education there was derailed, however, by the racism of his White classmates. "Nigger go home!" was scrawled on his door (Dyson, 1997). Traumatized by his experiences at Cranbrook, he failed out of school and found himself back at the same Detroit ghetto neighborhood he was hoping to flee.

Feeling humiliated and at a loss, his life's path took a series of dramatic turns. At 18 he became a father of a baby boy and was living on welfare. At 19 he became an ordained minister. While preaching he attended night school and earned his high school diploma. At 21 he entered Knoxville College and later transferred to Carson-Newman College, both in Tennessee. While in college, Dyson continued preaching in local churches. However, his stances against what he believed to be racist and sexist practices by these churches got him fired, twice (Dyson, 1995). He was first fired from a White church for questioning why church leaders didn't have more Black speakers and then fired from a Black church for enlisting women as deacons. These commitments to justice and equality, and his passionate responses to these commitments extend through his life's work. Dyson went on to attend Princeton where he earned his Masters and Doctorate degrees in religion, leading him to work

James D. Kirylo (Ed.), A Critical Pedagogy of Resistance: 34 Pedagogues We Need to Know, 37–40.

at a series of prestigious universities. Currently he is a professor at Georgetown University where he teaches theology, English, and African American Studies.

CRITICAL ECLECTIC THOUGHT

As of this writing, Michael Eric Dyson has produced 19 books on a vast array of topics and subjects ranging from Dr. Martin Luther King to Tupac Shakur, from Marvin Gaye to Bill Cosby. His own story of a young, black man growing up on the west side of Detroit in the 1970s and the hardships he and his family endured is frequently present in his work. He begins *Between God and Gangsta Rap: Bearing Witness to Black Culture* (Dyson, 1996) with a heart- wrenching letter to his brother Everett who is in prison, falsely convicted Dyson maintains, for murder. Dyson discusses the story of his brother Everett and its significance in terms of the racism embedded in the U.S. legal system and the numerous pathologies linked to the systematic denials of educational and economic opportunities to young low-income people of color (Dyson, 1995; 1996; 2002).

Whether he is writing about Tupak Shakur, Malcolm X, or Bill Cosby, Dyson often plays to the role of "Devil's" advocate pushing readers to explore subjects on race, class, gender, and sexual identity in complex ways and *always* with a passionate and resolute voice. In his writings about Dr. Martin Luther King and Malcolm X, for example, he lays out the dangers for an America seeking to deal with its legacy of racial oppression of boiling down their respective legacies to a set of simplified, out-of-context quotations, sound bites, and iconography (Dyson, 1995; 2000; 2008). In his book *April 4, 1968: Martin Luther King's Death and How it Changed America* (Dyson, 2008), Dyson urges America to expand their understandings of the civil rights leader's work, indeed his militancy, within the larger context of the American story. Although other curriculum scholars have made these similar arguments, Dyson's elaborations of the personal, political, even spiritual evolutions of figures such as Dr. King—as well as figures such as Malcolm X and Tupac Shakur, offer educators fuller, more complex portraits—including the flaws and inconsistencies— of his subjects *and* of understandings of race, class, gender, and sexual identity in America.

Dyson's unwavering commitment to equity and justice—was on display in the debate about the banning of ethnic studies in the State of Arizona (e.g., Cooper, 2010). Throughout these debates, Dyson offered spirited defenses of ethnic studies programs such as those enacted in Arizona. Opponents characterize such ethnic studies programs as "creating a hostile atmosphere in the school for other students" (Strauss, 2010). Dyson, however, countered that any efforts on the part of the state that prevents students from being exposed to, or studying histories of past oppression in the U.S., like the one signed into law by Arizona Governor Jan Brewer, is on its face racist.

Dyson's work also addresses White responses to civil rights legislation, including affirmative action programs, ethnic studies, bilingual education, and the schooling of immigrant children (Dyson, 1997; 2008). Dyson laments the ways these responses position beneficiaries of these legislative efforts as "advantaged" at the expense of Whites and that the defenders of these civil rights efforts are written off as politically naïve. In the end, much of Dyson's work clearly delineates the historical distortions even erasures that systematically deny the role of past racial and gender discrimination while at the same time denying the continued effects of this past on our current social and economic institutions, including schools.

Although Dyson works hard to make accessible his writings to a wider audience, he also stresses the importance of theory. Dyson understands the reasons some African-Americanist scholars spurn European theories and work on more traditional ways of analysis. But he offers two vital skills that can help theory better help explain and understand Black cultural experiences and expressions in America. The first skill is *translation*. What helps make meaning in one context, according to Dyson, must often be restated—but not over simplified—to help make sense in another context (Dyson, 1996; 2004). To interpret Black cultural productions, according to Dyson, the moral of the story (even if there is no moral) must be made clear. The subtleties and the nomenclature of theory must be made more apparent lest the theoretically uninitiated—namely low-income people of color under the figurative microscope—be left out (Dyson, 2004).

The second skill is *baptism*. Although he is well aware of the response this word evokes due to its religious connotations, he maintains that for cultural theorists like "Lyotard, Derrida, and Foucault to be of use, they can't be dragged whole-hog into Black intellectual debates without getting dipped into the waters of African-American culture" (Dyson, 1996, p. 133). Drawing on imagery of his faith, Dyson calls out for theory that is reborn in the waters of Black cultural expressions and productions such as jazz, hip hop, science fiction, collagist painting, and a range of other Black expressions and productions—embodied by folks such as Betty Carter, Snoop Doggy Dogg, Octavia Butler, Romair Bearden, and so many more. Dyson maintains that all of these folks' Black cultural expressions have something to gain from, and to give to, theory. Dyson takes his cue from Bertrand Russell to make his point: the goal of education is to help us resist the seductions of eloquence. For Dyson, theory at its best—in translation and baptized—can do just that (Dyson, 1996; 2004).

CONCLUSION

Michael Eric Dyson's work on race in America, as well as on class, gender, sexual identity, and hip-hop places him squarely in the company of other high profile scholars such as Henry Louis Gates, bell hooks, Cornell West and Patricia Williams. These scholars are part of a new generation of black public intellectuals who bring their many talents to address questions of public policy, in particular public policy that is of importance to African Americans. A self-described "homeboy with a Ph.D.," Dyson maintains that public intellectuals have a responsibility to be both self-critical and to do serious, rigorous work. However, public intellectuals also need to leave academia in order to speak to those who make decisions; to speak truth to power *and* the powerless with clarity and eloquence. And Michael Eric Dyson has been doing this since age eleven.

REFERENCES

Cooper, A. (2010). *Ethnic studies ban racist*? Retrieved from http://ac360.blogs.cnn.com/2010/05/13/must-see-ac360-az-ethnic-studies-discussion/

Dyson, M. E. (1995). *Making Malcolm: The myth and meaning of Malcolm X*, New York: Oxford University Press.

Dyson, M. E. (1996). *Race rules: Navigating the color line*, Reading, Massachusetts: Addison Wesley.

Dyson, M. E. (1997). *Between God and Gangsta rap: Bearing witness to black culture*, Oxford University Press, USA

Dyson, M. E. (2000). *I may not get there with you: The true Martin Luther King, Jr.*, New York: Free Press

Dyson, M. E. (2002). *Holler if you hear me: Searching for Tupac Shakur*, New York: Basic Civitas Books.

Dyson, M. E. (2004). *The Michael Eric Dyson reader*. New York: Basic Civitas Books.

Dyson, M. E. (2005). *Is Bill Cosby right?: Or gas the black middle class lost its mind*? New York: Basic Civitas Books.

Dyson, M. E. (2008). *April 4, 1968: Martin Luther King's death and how it changed America*, New York: Basic Civitas Books.

Strauss, V. (May 25, 2010). *Why Arizona targeted ethnic studies*. Washington Post. Retrieved from http://voices.washingtonpost.com/answer-sheet/civics-education/why-arizona-targeted-ethnic-st.html

MICHAEL E. LEE

11. IGNACIO ELLACURÍA

Historical Reality, Liberation, and the Role of the University

There he lay. Face down on the lawn with a bullet in his head. Along with the seminarians' cook, her daughter, and five of his fellow Jesuit priests, Ignacio Ellacuría was assassinated by members of the Salvadoran military's elite Atlacatl unit on November 16, 1989. In many ways, the killings that took place on the campus of the Jesuit-run Universidad Centroamericana José Simeón Cañas (UCA) were just another massacre in a decade-long civil war that had seen atrocities like these all too frequently. Ellacuría and the others died like so many other Salvadorans. Yet, these deaths were different in some way. This murder of Ellacuría, the university president, which took place on the university grounds, was precisely about the university and the role it had come to play in the nation, in the church, and in the larger geopolitical stage in which the Salvadoran civil war had taken a surprisingly central role.

Why was Ellacuría the primary target of an assassination? What was it about his philosophy and the UCA's work that would generate such furious hostility? How did a university become a target of military opposition so that the assassins would not only vandalize computers and books, but elect the symbolism of killing Ellacuría by splattering his brain on the blood-soaked ground? A brief sketch of Ellacuría's central ideas and summary of the UCA's activities during the war will both provide the preliminary answers to these complex questions and serve to introduce one of the most remarkable visionaries for the responsibilities and possibilities of the contemporary university.

PHILOSOPHER OF HISTORICAL REALITY

Though born in the Basque country of Spain, Ignacio Ellacuría was a naturalized Salvadoran citizen who first came to the small Central American country in 1949 as an eighteen year-old Jesuit seminary student. His training in philosophy and theology took him to Ecuador, Austria, and Spain, but Ellacuría always returned to El Salvador. In some sense, his thought never left El Salvador because he developed both his philosophy of historical reality and his liberation theology in response to the struggles of the poor majority of the country. This philosophy and theology would ground his ideas about the role of the university and guide its actions through the tumultuous civil war.

James D. Kirylo (Ed.), A Critical Pedagogy of Resistance: 34 Pedagogues We Need to Know, 41–44.

Ellacuría's philosophy, deeply influenced by that of his mentor, Xavier Zubiri, stems from the diagnosis of a basic flaw in much Western thought: philosophy misapprehends the basic act of human knowing by dividing sense and intellect, and this division has two disastrous consequences: 1) the intellect is divorced from reality and can only arrive at it through concepts; and, 2) reality itself is reduced to a thing or entity that loses its openness and dynamism. Rather than perpetuate a division between ideas (beyond reality) and sense-data (that we perceive), Ellacuría treats human intellection as a "sentient intelligence" that assumes that humans are installed in reality in a basic way and must confront the ethical demands of reality (Ellacuría, 1990). He emphasizes the interrelated character of all things, from their biological roots to the most complex structures that represent the historical actions of human beings. His philosophy of historical reality thus prioritizes placing oneself in the location that most fully reveals the truth about history in all its complexity: the world of the poor (Burke & Lassalle-Klein, 2006).

With roots in his philosophical vision prioritizing the marginalized and oppressed, and as part of the wave of thinking known as "liberation theology," Ellacuría articulates an understanding of Christian salvation as present in history in some way, revealed specifically as good news to the poor (Lee, 2013). Instead of dangerous separations such as theory-practice, body-soul, or heaven-earth, Ellacuría's theology possesses an incarnational imagination in which God's transcendence is "in" and not "away from" history (Lee, 2009). Christian faith must respond not simply by seeking an afterlife, but transforming the world so that it more clearly reveals the transcendent presence of God. It is with this vision of human intelligence and its ethical demands that Ellacuría grounds the vision for the university carried out at the UCA.

A UNIVERSITY WITH A CENTER OUTSIDE ITSELF

Originally founded in 1965, the UCA was viewed by the Salvadoran elite as a conservative haven from so-called secular and Marxist-inspired academics of the national university. Yet, under the leadership of Ellacuría, the UCA transformed in the 1970s and 80s into one of the most outspoken critics of the brutal military regimes that governed El Salvador and of the social, political, and economic structures that undergirded the massive inequality that characterized Salvadoran society. This transformation sprang from the UCA's commitment to serve the national reality, but to do so *universitáriamente*, in the distinct manner of a university.

If the university is the cultivator of truth and knowledge, Ellacuría reasoned, it does so not in an abstract fashion but in a real, historical way. The existence of extensive poverty and oppression represent a historical negation of truth and reason that demands analysis and resistance. In an unjust society, the university must function to study reality and uncover the truth so that it can participate in interpreting and transforming the ideological frameworks that sustain the unjust status quo. In other words, Ellacuría believed that a university cannot simply dedicate itself to the production of professionals or technicians who replicate the social structures already in place, nor commit itself to an abstract and a-historical quest for knowledge, which divorced from the reality of immense inequality serves only to reinforce its ideological bases. Rather, in a favorite phrase of Ellacuría's, the university should serve as the "critical and creative conscience of society." He splits the Spanish word for conscience *con-cienca* (lit., 'with-learning') to indicate the manner that the university analyzes causes, discovers remedies, and communicates a consciousness (Beirne, 1996).

In this vision of the university, teaching and research are linked by a third unifying element: what Ellacuría calls *proyección social* ("social projection"). Social projection makes concrete the orientation of the university to the wider society and indicates how the university must have a center "outside itself," where that which is most conducive to satisfying the needs of the poor majority serves as the criterion and principle for determining research priorities and other university functions. Practically, social projection indicates the various ways that the university "projects" its knowledge to the wider society, but also allows the society, and particularly its poorest, to orient its activities (Brackley, 2008).

THE UNIVERSITY AMIDST A NATIONAL CRISIS

During the last decade of Ellacuría's life, a period that coincides with his presidency of the UCA, the 'social projection' of the university faced its greatest challenge: the descent of the country into civil war.

The first half of that decade demanded confrontation with the propaganda and ideological interests of powerful forces, primarily a Reagan State Department that clamored for military support for the Salvadoran government because it viewed Central America as the pivotal battleground in the fight against Soviet global expansion. As civilian casualties mounted, Ellacuría was convinced that a real solution to the war could not be achieved through a military victory by either side. In publications and speaking engagements, Ellacuría and the UCA criticized U.S. intervention by denouncing inflated election numbers used to sway foreign policy and exposing the savagery of the Low Intensity Conflict military strategy (Whitfield, 1995). At the same time, the UCA did not hesitate from denouncing the guerrilla Farabundo Martí National Liberation Front's strategic shift to a war of attrition, characterized by damage to infrastructure, political kidnappings, and assassinations.

By the middle of the 1980s, the UCA emerged as the leading independent source of information about El Salvador's political, economic, and social reality. For foreign journalists and other newcomers, it was often a shock to see a Catholic priest function as an expert on the socio-political circumstances of the nation. As part of its social projection, the UCA developed key institutes, such as the Human Rights Institute (IDHUCA), which documented kidnappings, torture, massacres, and other abuses, the Institute of Public Opinion (IUDOP), which conducted urban and rural surveys on various topics, and Ellacuría's own brainchild, the UCA's, Seminar on

National Reality, which was the only forum where leading figures in the conflict could debate the issues openly (Hasset & Lacey, 1991).

These institutes gave flesh to social projection and moved beyond the propaganda of the warring parties to document the great suffering of the nation and bring its reality to the awareness of the world. Tragically, the UCA paid the price for its social projection. Threats, periods of exile, and bombings of the campus culminated on that fateful November night when Ellacuría and the others, known collectively as the "UCA martyrs," offered their last testimony to what the university can and should be.

REFERENCES

Beirne, C. J. (1996). *Jesuit education and social change in El Salvador*. New York: Garland Publishing, Inc.

Brackley, D. (2008). *The university and its martyrs: Hope from central America*. San Salvador: Centro Monseñor Romero/UCA Editores.

Burke, K., & Lassalle-Klein, R. (2006). *Love that produces hope: The thought of Ignacio Ellacuría*. Collegeville, MN: Liturgical Press.

Ellacuría, I. (1999). *Escritos universitarios*. San Salvador: UCA Editores.

Ellacuría, I. (1990). *Filosofía de la realidad histórica*. San Salvador: UCA Editores.

Hassett, J., & Lacey, H. (1991). *Towards a society that serves its people: The intellectual contribution of El Salvador's murdered Jesuits*. Washington, D.C.: Georgetown University Press.

Lee, M. (2009). *Bearing the weight of salvation: The soteriology of Ignacio Ellacuría*. New York: Crossroad Publishing, Inc.

Lee, M. (Ed.). (2013). *Ignacio Ellacuría: Essays on history, liberation and salvation*. Maryknoll, NY: Orbis Books.

Whitfield, T. (1995). *Paying the price: Ignacio Ellacuría and the murdered Jesuits of El Salvador*. Philadelphia: Temple University Press.

SANDRA J. STONE

12. ANA MARIA ARAÚJO FREIRE

Scholar, Humanitarian, and Carrying on Paulo Freire's Legacy

Ana Maria Araújo (Nita) Freire was born in Recife, Brazil, November 13, 1933. Her parents were educators at the Colégio Osvaldo Cruz and guided her in ethical, scientific, and moral education. The high school she attended was owned by her parents, Genove and Aluizio Pessia de Araújo. In college, she majored in pedagogy, then obtained a Master's degree (1988) and a Ph.D. (1994) in education at the Pontificia Universidade Católica de São Paulo (PUC/SP), Brazil. Her focus was the history of illiteracy in Brazil (The Paulo and Nita Freire International Project for Critical Pedagogy, 2007).

Nita is a historian, writer, researcher, and teacher in her own right. She has written books, articles and book chapters. She has lectured throughout the world, including Europe, Latin America, and the United States. She taught history of education at colleges and universities in the city of São Paulo for many years. However, it is impossible to speak about Nita Freire's work without speaking of her second husband, Paulo Freire. Nita first met Paulo when she was almost four years old, and he was 16 and a student at her father's high school. Thus, began parallel lives that united in marriage in 1988 after the loss of her first husband, Raul, and Paulo's first wife, Elza. Nita recalls that, indeed, Paulo always had a certain presence in her life (Germano & Reigota, 2006). During his youth, Nita's parents were influential in guiding Paulo to be a humanist and in "being human," a reality she lived as well. Without the determination of Paulo's mother as she begged for a scholarship for her son, and the generosity of Nita's father, it would have been impossible for Paulo to attend an excellent school and eventually write his seminal work, *Pedagogy of the Oppressed* (Macedo, 2001. Introduction section, p. 6, as cited in A. Freire, 2001).

Paulo taught Portuguese at the Oswaldo Cruz School and was Nita's teacher when she was in her first year of high school at age 11. Their parallel lives continued to touch from time to time. In 1979, she welcomed Paulo back to Brazil from exile. Then, in 1985, a widowed Nita returned to PUC/SP for her graduate work where Paulo became her academic advisor for her doctoral studies on the history of illiteracy in Brazil. This last encounter led to a union of love and marriage in 1988, steering the both of them on an amazing journey of partnership and collaboration. Nita embraced Paulo's mission in life. As one of the most important influential educators in the last half century, he was devoted to the liberation of the oppressed, and believed in the *possibility* of transforming society through a vision that was rooted in hope (P. Freire, 1996; A. Freire, 2001; Germano & Reigota, 2006; Kirylo, 2011).

James D. Kirylo (Ed.), A Critical Pedagogy of Resistance: 34 Pedagogues We Need to Know, 45–48.

COLLABORATOR, SCHOLAR, HUMANITARIAN, AND HISTORIAN

Nita Freire solidified her place in the history of important pedagogues as she entered her collaborative work with Paulo Freire after their marriage. Her background, experience, understanding, and passion made her uniquely qualified to pursue this journey. Paulo said she was one of very few people who understood his work, noting that she understood his ideas better than he did (A. Freire, 2001). Nita wrote detailed endnotes for Paulo's books, including *Pedagogy of Hope* (1994), *Teachers as Cultural Workers* (1998), *Pedagogy of the Heart* (2007) and *Letters to Cristina* (1996). After his death in 1997, she organized three of Paulo's books: *Pedagogy of Indignation* (2004), *Daring to Dream: Toward a Pedagogy of the Unfinished* (2006), and *Pedagogia da tolerancia* (2005) (not yet translated into English). In addition, Nita wrote *Chronicles of Love: My Life with Paulo Freire* in 2001, and Paulo's biography, *Paulo Freire: Uma Historia de Vida* in 2006 (not yet translated into English), which won second place in the 2007 Prêmio Jabuti, a most prestigious Brazilian literary award under the category of "Best Biography" (Kirylo, 2011; Nita Freire's Autobiography, retrieved from http://www.freireproject.org).

As an historian, Nita meticulously highlighted the context of Paulo's work. Context, where he was from, defined him. For example, in her endnotes for *Letters to Cristina* (1996), she read the *world* to analyze, reflect, and frame the *word*. She illuminated the setting and the issues, making the context more dynamic, providing depth and affect. She detailed the socio-political structure in Brazil before and after Paulo's years of exile. She humanized the tortured, the oppressed. She voiced the torturers' deprivation of humanity and lit the way to see that freedom is the center of being human (P. Freire, 1996).

Nita provided statistics that underscored the plight of the oppressed as in the case for the endnotes in *Pedagogy of the Heart* (2007) where she highlights the overwhelming number of 130,000 inmates in 297 correctional facilities, 500,000 girls as prostitutes on Brazilian streets, 32 million people starving, and 7 million people suffering from physical or mental illness. She enlarged the battle against sociopolitical injustice. As she noted, she never tried to interfere with the dialogue between Paulo and his readers, but used her descriptions, narratives and reflections to clarify the context (P. Freire, 2007). Indeed, Paulo wrote that Nita's "keen understanding of history enabled her to make compelling arguments concerning the importance of rethinking those historical contexts that had radicalized my thinking and that had given birth to *Pedagogy of Hope: A Reencounter with Pedagogy of the Oppressed*" (Macedo, 2001, Introduction section, p. 4, as cited in A. Freire, 2001).

In her detailed narratives, Nita was not content to just give the facts; she elaborated and reflected on the contexts and information, without invading Paulo's text, giving ideas their own soul and autonomy (A. Freire, 1996, Notes section, p. 1, as cited in P. Freire, 1996). In an effort to complement his work, she took his words and ideas beyond the local level to the universal public square (P. Freire, 2007). For example, in *Letters to Cristina* (1996), she voiced strong opposition to school grade retention, which is very high in Brazil. Children who are held back at the very beginning of the school experience, she lamented was unjust and cruel. She understood that these children would probably never return to school and never have the opportunity to read and write. The high rate of retention during the second phase of elementary education was nothing less than elitism. Also in her notes in *Letters to Cristina*, she provides a substantive discourse on hunger, passionately denouncing the scandalous nature of it. In a democracy, she declared that everyone should have the right to eat, and the degrading stigma of hunger must be eliminated (A. Freire, 1996, Notes section, pp. 230–248, as cited in P. Freire, 1996).

NITA FREIRE AS A LEGACY FOR PAULO

Nita stands alone as academic, activist, and advocate for the oppressed. However, Nita gave up her personal work as a professor to be close to Paulo and to work and study with him for their 10 years together. They treasured their love for each other and the opportunities to be together (Borg & Mayo, 2000). After Paulo's first wife Elza's death, he lost his desire to live. Nita renewed his hopes, his joy, his dreams – and most of all, the possibility to love again. He tenderly wrote, ". . . Because you gave me direction when I had lost my address, because you brought me life when I wilted away, because you gave meaning to my meaninglessness. I love you jealously . . ." (A. Freire, 2001, pp. 76–77). Because of her inseparable, loving relationship to Paulo combined with her extraordinary historical and academic background, she is the most esteemed Freirean scholar today. Her intellectual gifts sustain her ability to carry Paulo's torch (Macedo, 2001, Introduction section, p. 6, as cited in A. Freire, 2001), and her passion for justice roots her to continue his legacy in the move toward a more free, democratic, loving world.

Nita Freire participates in The Paulo and Nita Freire International Project for Critical Pedagogy established in 2007 at McGill University, Canada.

REFERENCES

Borg, C., & Mayo, P. (2000). Reflections from a "third age" marriage. A pedagogy of hope, reason, and passion: An interview with Ana Maria (Nita) Araujo Freire. *McGill Journal of Education, 35*(2).
Freire, A. (2001). *Chronicles of love: My life with Paulo Freire*. New York, NY: Peter Lang.
Freire, P. (1996). *Letters to Cristina: Reflections on my life and work*. New York, NY: Routledge.
Freire, P. (2007). *Pedagogy of the heart*. New York, NY: Continuum.
Germano, M. A., & Reigota, M. (2006). *Remembering Paulo Freire: Ten years without him: Interview with Dr. Ana Maria Araujo Freire* (Translated by V. Rodrigues). Retrieved from www.freireproject.org/content/nita-freire
Kirylo, J. D. (2011). *Paulo Freire: The man from Recife*. New York, NY: Peter Lang.
Macedo, D. (2001). Introduction. In A. Freire (Ed.), *Chronicles of love: My life with Paulo Freire* (pp. 1–9). New York, NY: Peter Lang.
The Paulo and Nita Freire International Project for Critical Pedagogy. (2007). Retrieved from http://www.freireproject.org

JAMES D. KIRYLO

13. PAULO FREIRE

"Father" of Critical Pedagogy

INTRODUCTION

One of the most important critical pedagogues the world has seen in the last 100 years, Paulo Freire is that rare person who emerges every so often in critical points of history when there is a need of a courageous, prophetic voice of conscience. Extraordinarily grounded in the wisdom of humility, yet gifted with remarkable strength, deep insight and perceptive intelligence, Freire was profoundly committed to challenge individuals and institutional structures that perpetuated the status quo.

Born in Recife, Brazil, Paulo Reglus Neves Freire grew up in what he describes as a middle-class family, which was notably marked by the fact that his father regularly wore a tie to work, and that the family lived in a house owned by his uncle, and one that was modestly furnished, particularly so by a family owned German piano. Paulo, however, lived what he describes as a "connective kid," meaning that those symbolic middle-class markers simply enabled him to connect with others who were considered middle-class, but in reality he deeply identified with the poor, experiencing acute hunger and poverty (Freire, 1996).

Paulo was raised in a loving home environment where his parents fostered a dialogical environment, and where he learned to read and write from them in their backyard under the shadow of a mango tree. Paulo's father died when he was only 13 years old, and despite the devastating loss and economic hardships, his mother worked extraordinarily hard in seeking a good school high school for Paulo. Her dedicated efforts marvelously materialized when Dr. Aluízio Pessoa de Araújo, the director of Colégio Oswaldo Cruz (Oswaldo Cruz Secondary School) in Recife, kindly accepted Paulo to attend the school for free. It was from there that Paulo excelled in Brazilian Portuguese, which he eventually taught at the school. At the same time he studied law, and later on went into practice only to give it up after his first client (Freire, 1996, 1994a).

Turning his full-time attention to education, he began his work with various positions at the Serviço Social da Indústria (SESI) and other agencies, which enabled him to work on numerous social and education programs in Northeast Brazil. It was from this rich experience he observed how unjust policies kept masses of people from equal opportunity and access. In response, Freire went on to promote a highly successful literacy program for adult literacy learners, which empowered thousands

James D. Kirylo (Ed.), A Critical Pedagogy of Resistance: 34 Pedagogues We Need to Know, 49–52.

to come out from what he describes as a "culture of silence" enabling them to participate more fully in voicing how injustice was institutionally perpetrated (Freire 1996, 1985).

Disturbingly catching the attention of the establishment for his innovative approach to adult literacy learning, Freire was questioned, thrown into jail, and was forced into exile in 1964, sending him on a 16 year odyssey that took him to Bolivia, Chile, Harvard, and onto the World Council of Churches in Geneva, Switzerland. It was during his exile experience that Freire naturally landed on the world stage, particularly heightened by the publication of his seminal work, *Pedagogy of the Oppressed*, which is perhaps the best and most concise presentation of the critical aspects of Freire's philosophy (Roberts, 2000). Through an amnesty program, Freire returned for good back to Brazil in 1980.

Paulo's first wife, Elza, was a powerful force in his life, and birthed their five children. With her passing, Paulo experience his dark night of the soul, only to experience an ecstasy of new life with his marriage to Ana Maria (Nita) who remained his companion and collaborator until his death in 1997. Often referred to as the inaugural protagonist of critical pedagogy, Freire is the author of numerous books and articles which have been translated in a variety of languages (McLaren, 2000).

CRITICAL TENETS OF THOUGHT

Paulo Freire characterized himself as a "tramp of the obvious," meaning the starting point of his work began with an examination of obvious realities (e.g., illiteracy, joblessness, hunger, etc.). And, he found it simultaneously amusing and disturbing that his reporting of obvious realities not only attracted attention, but also garnered him reproach, which ultimately signaled to him the power of the hegemonic forces at work (Freire, 1985). Therefore, movement toward transformative change is fostered in a counter–hegemonic process where one does not escape from history, but rather embraces and acts in history as subject. In other words and particularly revolutionary for those who have historically been living in the shadows, history does not need to be fixed or predetermined; rather history is a possibility; it can be made, invented and reinvented (Freire, 1997). The engagement of those who have been historically marginalized in their movement toward becoming subject is rooted in Freire's conviction that humanization (or becoming more fully human) is an ontological vocation and implies the political nature embedded in the process and the non-neutrality of its practice (Freire, 1994a, 1990).

For Freire, there are fundamentally two broad approaches to pedagogical practice. The first is what he describes as a banking education, which is driven by the assumptions that people are manageable and adaptable; the teacher sees reality as compartmentalized and one that is static and predictable; students learn through memorization as per what is dictated by the teacher; and, a dichotomy exists between a person and the world. And because the cultural–socio–historical setting is not contextualized, the existential reality of the learner is not a consideration, which thwarts creativity, reinforces a fatalistic outlook, and functions through a monologue or anti–dialogical stance (Freire, 1990).

The antithesis of a banking approach is what Freire characterizes as a problem–posing education. In this approach, the driving assumptions are that people are viewed as conscious beings who are unfinished, but yet are in the process of becoming; liberation occurs through cognitive acts as opposed to the transfer of information (Freire, 1990). A problem–posing approach unfolds in a dialogical setting, which is not to say that dialogue is simply a "conversation" or a mere sharing of ideas. Rather, embedded in the element of dialogue is criticality in problematizing the existential reality of the subject, a process in which students are presented with problems relative to their relationship with the world, leading them to be challenged yet prompted to respond to that challenge within a context of other interrelated problems (Freire, 1990, 1985).

Dialogue and the notion of praxis (the dialectical interweaving of theory and practice) cultivates Freire's concept of conscientização (conscientization) which is an unfolding process that is filtered through a contextual framework that intersects the psychological–political–theological–social milieu in the awakening of critical awareness (Freire, 1994b). The notion of conscientization is not static or formulaic, but rather is situated in historical spaces and times, implying that the process is not a blueprint to indicate how it unfolds for every individual regardless of their society, location, and era (Freire, 1994b, Roberts, 2000).

With an insatiable desire to learn from the beginning to the end of his life, Paulo Freire drew from a wide range of existential thinkers, understanding himself as a human being thoughtfully under construction, continuously reinventing his life and work. In that light, he saw life as something that was not predetermined and was intensely aware of his "unfinishedness" and to remain inert was not an option; that is, his "epistemological curiosity" was driven by the dialectic of what he knew and what he didn't know and, thus, the desire to be in a continuous, evolving process of learning, growing, and changing (Freire, 2007; 1998). The brilliance of Freire's pedagogy of "unfinishedness" was that he possessed the perceptive insight to draw from a diverse range of influences and logically blend them into a unifying educational philosophy, which has led scholars and practitioners from around the world to uniquely identify a way of thinking or teaching that would fall under the singular umbrella of Freirean thought or Freirean action (Kirylo, 2011).

Proclaimed by law as Patrono da Educação No Brasil (Patron of Education in Brazil) by government officials in 2012, Paulo Freire remained unwavering in his life's work toward cultivating the betterment of humanity where ultimately oppression would cease and a culture of silence would no longer exist. Freire's prophetic vision of hope saw a more just world, a more democratic society, a place that would celebrate differences, and a people who would live among each other in respect, love, and freedom.

REFERENCES

Freire, P. (2007). *Daring to dream: Toward a pedagogy of the unfinished.* (Organized and presented by Ana Maria Araújo Freire). (Translated by Alexandre K. Oliveira). Boulder, CO: Paradigm Publishers.

Freire, P. (1998). *Pedagogy of freedom: Ethics, democracy, and civic courage.* Lanham, MD: Rowman and Littlefield Publishers, Inc.

Freire, P. (1997). A response. In P. Freire, J.W. Fraser, D. Macedo, T. McKinnon, & W.T. Stokes (Eds.), *Mentoring the mentor: A critical dialogue with Paulo Freire* (pp. 303–329). New York, NY: Peter Lang.

Freire, P. (1996). *Letters to Cristina: Reflections on my life and work* (D. Macedo with Q. Macedo and A. Oliveira, Trans.). New York, NY: Routledge.

Freire, P. (1994a). *Pedagogy of hope: Reliving pedagogy of the oppressed.* (Robert R. Barr, Trans.). New York, NY: Continuum.

Freire, P. (1994b). *Education for critical consciousness.* New York, NY: Continuum.

Freire, P. (1990). *Pedagogy of the oppressed.* New York, NY: Continuum.

Freire, P. (1985). The *politics of education: Culture, power, and liberation.* New York, NY: Bergin & Garvey.

Kirylo, J. D. (2011). *Paulo Freire: The man from Recife.* New York, NY: Peter Lang.

Roberts, P. (2000). *Education, literacy, and humanization: Exploring the work of Paulo Freire.* Westport, Connecticut: Bergin & Garvey.

McLaren, P. (2000). *Che Guevara, Paulo Freire, and the pedagogy of revolution.* Lanham MD: Rowman & Littlefield Publishers, Inc.

KENNEDY O. ONGAGA

14. HENRY LOUIS GATES, JR.

Prolific Writer and Proponent of African-American Literature

BACKGROUND

Henry Louis Gates Jr. is a leading academic and cultural critic in the United States. Born in September, 1950 in Keyser, West Virginia, Gates was raised in a supportive household. While his father worked two jobs as a paper mill worker and as a janitor at a telephone company, Gates' mother cleaned houses and was very involved in the education of her two children. In fact, she was the first black woman in her community to be elected as PTA president. Gates remembers his father as an extraordinary storyteller and credits his mother for imbuing in him and his brother a great sense of self-confidence, value of education, and purpose in life. At the age of 14, Gates suffered a hairline fracture of the ball-and-socket joint of his hip while playing touch football, which was misdiagnosed by the doctor. As a consequent, his right leg is more than two inches shorter than his left, leading him to walk with the aid of cane as he does to this date.

Gates, Jr. grew up during the era of Jim Crow and the emerging civil rights movement, which shaped his racial consciousness and deeply influenced his later literary works. After receiving a degree in English Language and Literature, *Summa cum laude*, from Yale in 1973, Gates went on to earn a M.A. and Ph.D. in English Literature from Clare College at the University of Cambridge in 1979. Gates was the university's first African American to earn a Ph.D., and while conducting his graduate studies, he studied under the tutelage of Nobel laureate Nigerian playwright Wole Soyinka with whom he shared common "sensibility" rather than an "ethnicity." It was Soyinka who convinced Gates to study literature, specifically African-American literature and its lineage to the literary traditions of Africa and the Caribbean (Gale, 2008). Gates went on to teach at Cornell, Duke, and Yale, and is currently the Alphonse Fletcher University Professor, director of the W.E.B. Du Bois Institute for African and African American Research, and chair of the Afro-American Studies Department at Harvard University.

AFRICAN-AMERICAN LITERATURE, HISTORY, AND CULTURE

A prolific writer, Gates is the author/co-author and editor/co-editor of numerous books, and has written numerous articles, including those in popular magazines such as *The New Yorker*, *Time*, and *The New Republic*. Gates' literary works are primarily

James D. Kirylo (Ed.), A Critical Pedagogy of Resistance: 34 Pedagogues We Need to Know, 53–56.

centered on bringing to light lost and hidden African American experience, including identity, culture, race, history, and multiculturalism.

In his memoir, *Colored People* (1994), Gates reflects on his childhood experience in West Virginia and attempts to portray the intricate ways black culture is embedded in the practices of everyday life and a world shifting from segregation to integration and from colored to Negro to black. He reveals that his personal statement in his application to Yale indicated that his grandfather was colored, his father was Negro, and he is black. The use of these terms—colored, Negro, and black—not only mark different users and frameworks of time and place, but also demonstrate Gates' quest for African American identity – who we are and how we are labeled by both ourselves and others. By so doing, Gates explores and provides us with a rich understanding of how nuances of language and identity shape each other, how labels and discourses shift and change based on speaker, audience, and context, and how those changes impact the real world.

Gates' fundamental argument in much of his literary works revolves around resurrecting, analyzing, understanding, and accepting African American literary, historical, and cultural discourses as part of the larger American story. Particularly heightened during the struggle for civil rights, Gates observed how African Americans were viewed as incapable of mastering "the arts and sciences" (Jaehn, 1998). In response to this bigoted thinking, Gates uses his intellectual prowess to advance the struggle of African American writers to define themselves, their craft, and their culture. He contends in *Figures in Black* (1987) that Afro-American literary tradition was generated as a response to eighteenth- and nineteenth-century allegations that persons of African descent did not, and could not, create literature. He is credited for the discovery, authentication, and publication of African American historical texts, including the 1859 autobiographical slave narrative, *Our Nig: Sketches from the Life of a Free Black* by Harriet E. Wilson and *The Bondwoman's Narrative,* a novel by Hannah Crafts, which scholars speculate was set in the mid-19th century and possibly the first written by an African-American woman.

In Gates' view, standard literary theories drawn from Western tradition are inadequate to interpret African American history and literature (Nickell, n.d.). He argues that African American tradition should be considered on "its own terms" and be allowed to speak in "its own voice." He seeks to uncover a unique system of rhetoric to help reveal and interpret a rich vernacular tradition that black slaves brought with them to the New World. Some of his works, *Loose Canons: Notes on the Culture Wars* (1992), a collection of previously published essays on aspects of multiculturalism in America, and *The Signifying Monkey: A Theory of Afro-American Literacy Criticism* (1988), advocate for the acknowledgement of an African American canon in America's mainstream literature as one way of shaping a truly common public culture, one responsive to the long-silenced cultures of color (Contemporary Black Biography, 2008).

Gates cautions that efforts to define African American canon should not be decried as racist, separatist, nationalist, or essentialist. Instead, he posits that the only way to transcend these divisions and forge a civic culture that respects both differences and similarities, is through education that respects both the diversity and commonalities of human culture. He observes that American society can only survive if it embraces the values of cultural tolerance, which emerge from cultural understanding.

An ardent believer that knowing thy ancestors is knowing thyself, and as a way of raising social consciousness and deconstructing African American traditions in mainstream America, Gates delved into genealogical research and genetic mapping project to track down his family tree and those of prominent African Americans, like Oprah Winfrey, Whoopi Goldberg and Quincy Jones (DeLuca, 2012). He presents his findings in a series of televised PBS documentaries, including In Search of Our Roots (2007) and America Beyond the Color Line (2004). The remarkable, yet unsettling revelations and gripping narratives that form the heart of these documentaries offer unprecedented insights that encompass the liberating strength and pride of African Americans and make American history intimate, concrete and personal. What he unlocks connects people to their past and demonstrates the diversity of American people, who they are and where they come from. For instance, an examination of his heritage revealed that his genetic profile matched people in Ireland, and that he had a Black ancestor who fought in the American Revolutionary War.

Gates' use of genomic research and DNA technology has the potential to *blur* racial boundaries by showing groups to be indistinct or mixed, or *sharpen* racial lines by revealing a person's ancestral homogeneity or pointing toward a particular set of forebears (Hochschild & Sen, 2012). In Gates' view, doing family trees adds specificity to the raw data from which historians can generalize about the complexity of the American experience. At the same time, it shows both the remarkable extent of inter-racial mixing during slavery, as well as the fact that "race" extends far beyond our skin color.

CONCLUSION

As a contemporary scholar and thinker, Gates continues to use his scholarly skills to reinvigorate the missing and long-neglected aspects of African-American experience and the building of a more pluralistic society. Because of his untiring efforts, Gates is the recipient of many honorary degrees and prestigious awards. Indeed, in large part because of Gates' work, African American Studies continues to gain recognition as a critically important field of study in American history.

REFERENCES

Contemporary Black Biography. (2008). *Henry Louis Gates Jr.* Retrieved from Encylopedia.com: http://www.encyclopedia.com/doc/1G2–3027700022.html

DeLuca, M. (2012, April 15). Henry Louis Gates, Jr. Reveals Rick Warren's Slave-Holding Ancestors. *The Daily Beast.* Retrieved from http://www.thedailybeast.com/articles/2012/04/15/henry-louis-gates-jr-unearths-rick-warren-s-slave-holding-ancestors.html

Gale. (2008). Henry Louis Gates Jr. *Contemporary Black Biography.* Vol. 67. Retrieved from http://www.gale.cengage.com/free_resources/bhm/bio/gates_h.htm

Gates, Jr., H. L. (1987). *Figures in Black: Words, Signs, and the "Racial" Self.* New York: Oxford University Press.

Gates, Jr., H. L. (1988). *The signifying monkey: A theory of Afro-American literary criticism.* Oxford: Oxford University Press.

Gates, Jr., H. L. (1992). *Loose Canons: Notes on the Culture Wars.* New York: Oxford University Press.

Gates, Jr., H. L. (1994). *Colored People: A Memoir.* New York: Alfred A. Knopf.

Gates, Jr., H. L. (2007). *In Search of Our Roots: How 19 Extraordinary African Americans Reclaimed Their Past.* New York: Crown Publishing Group.

Gates, H.L, Jr. (2004). *America beyond the color line with Henry Louis Gates, Jr.* In J. Hewes, & S. Chinn (Producers), & D. Percival, & M. Crisp, M (Directors). (DVD). USA: PBS.

Hochschild, J. & Sen, M. (2012, February). *Sharpening or blurring: the impact of genomic ancestry testing on Americans' racial identity.* Government Department: Harvard University. Retrieved from http://projects.iq.harvard.edu/genomics/files/the_impact_of_genomic_ancestry_testing_on_americans_racial_identity.pdf

Jaehn, T. (1998). *Henry Louis Gates Jr.:* Stanford Presidential Lectures in Humanities and Arts. Stanford University, CA. Retrieved from http://prelectur.stanford.edu/lecturers/gates/

Nickell, A. (n.d.). *Teaching African American literature.* Retrieved from http://www.uncp.edu/home/hickss/taal/overview/index.html

PBS.org. (2012, April). *Finding your roots with Henry Louis Gates, Jr.* Retrieved from http://www.pbs.org/wnet/finding-your-roots/video/

KATHLEEN E. FITE & JOVITA M. ROSS-GORDON

15. CAROL GILLIGAN

Critical Voice of Feminist Thought

BACKGROUND

Carol Gilligan's innovative contributions to moral development theory and her analysis of the influences of patriarchy on women, girls, and boys position her as a critical pedagogue. As an educator, researcher, psychologist, author, feminist, and advocate she continues to influence how the voices of women and men are heard and valued. Born in 1936 in New York City to William Friedman, a lawyer, and Mabel Caminez Friedman, a humanitarian, she experienced her parents' ethics of care, especially as they helped refugees who had fled Europe. She attended Walden School in New York City, a progressive school where issues related to morality and ethics were discussed, and Swarthmore College, where she received honors in English Literature. She completed a master's degree in clinical psychology from Radcliffe College; earned a Ph.D. in social psychology from Harvard University where she taught; and, also taught at the University of Chicago. At New York University she was affiliated with the Steinhardt School of Culture, Education and Human Development, the Graduate School of Arts and Science, and the School of Law, where she focused her attention on social justice activities (Goldberg, 2000; New York University School of Law, 2012).

CRITICAL WORKS

As a social and political activist during the 1960s and 1970s, Gilligan was involved with issues related to the draft, voter registration, civil rights, the antinuclear movement, and the women's strike for peace (Goldberg, 2000). She was drawn to the work of Erik Erikson and Lawrence Kohlberg because of their interest in psychology and commitment to civil rights and the antiwar movement. Her work as a research and teaching assistant for Lawrence Kohlberg drew her attention to an omission of a feminine perspective in his research on moral development. This led her on a path to critically examine gender differences with respect to moral development, ultimately opening the door to further research in feminine thought.

Gilligan's seminal work, *In A Different Voice* (1982), which continues to remain in print and has been translated into numerous languages, brought attention to keystones of moral and personal development and how they vary between men

James D. Kirylo (Ed.), A Critical Pedagogy of Resistance: 34 Pedagogues We Need to Know, 57–60.

and women, with female development focused more on relationships, attachment, and communication. This presence of feminist thought was a break from the mainstream of writing that focused on male development. Some of her work has been challenged because it was based on white, middle-class, heterosexual women, without acknowledgement that women who differ in race, class, religion, or sexual orientation might have different moral perspectives rooted in their life experiences. Also, her association between women and the ethic of care has attracted criticism for perpetuating the stereotypical social role of the traditional, full-time wife (Gould, 1988; Meece & Daniels, 2008). Yet, her later contributions clearly take a more critical turn.

In *Women, Girls, & Psychotherapy: Reframing Resistance,* Gilligan, Rogers, and Tolman (1991) analyze the societal forces that prompt adolescent girls to silence their inner voices and, therefore, "forget what they know." They also examine the ways girls resist psychologically and politically through their actions, even when those actions carry risks. Addressing feminist concerns about speaking in essentialist ways about gender, based only on studies of white middle class women and girls, Gilligan and a group of racially diverse colleagues conducted the multi-year "Understanding Adolescence Study" with a racially and ethnically diverse sample of inner-city girls. First, Gilligan and her associates held a series of Women and Race retreats aimed at helping them become more skilled in listening to the girls and interpreting their stories. They interviewed ethnically diverse working class girls between eighth and tenth grade and found them to be engaged in psychological dissociation and political resistance similar to that described in earlier studies with middle class girls. Dissociation was evidenced when they appeared to lose knowledge or feelings expressed when they were younger, sometimes responding as if they did not know or have an answer. Girls were seen as risking psychological distress if, in an attempt to comply, they give up meaningful personal relationships, or risking being at odds with the powers that be if they engage in overt acts of political resistance (Taylor, Gilligan, & Sullivan, 1997).

Teaming with David Richards, with whom she co-taught a seminar on gender and democracy at New York University, Gilligan co-authored *The Deepening Darkness: Patriarchy, Resistance, and Democracy's Future* (2009). They organized this volume into three parts, first describing increasing patriarchy and sexual repression and diminishing democracy in the ancient Roman Empire; then examining manifestations of sexism, racism, homophobia and other forms of oppression and resistance to these forces across cultures and centuries; and, finally speculating regarding democracy's future in the midst of contemporary political and social dilemmas. Gillian continues with the thesis of *The Deepening Darkness*—that the future of democracy depends on resistance to patriarchy—in her next work, *Joining the Resistance* (2011). Here she draws on her personal experiences and observations as a researcher as well as on literary works such as *The Diary of Anne Frank* and *The Scarlet Letter* to narrate the evolution of her ideas and research. She also includes the voices of boys who, as they enter high school, speak warmly of the value of relationships with their best friends though later, by the end of high school, they speak of relationships with others in the ways expected of men in patriarchal societies.

CONCLUSION

As the recipient of numerous awards and recognitions, such as being named one of the 25 most influential Americans by *Time* magazine, Gilligan has been extraordinarily influential in shaping feminist thought and helping us to better understand the human condition. Her work leads us to question the narrow reference to masculine or feminine because doing so encourages division and alienation when she suggests that what we should be seeking is a more universal desire for love and freedom (Gilligan, 2011). We are drawn by her work to question why and how we silence the voices of boys and girls, to imagine ways to help us learn to recover our voices that have been suppressed, and to embrace the use and respect of voice. Our schools and families serve as influential cornerstones for development. She reminds us that positive interactions among children of all ages and between children and their teachers and other adults is essential to a democratic society and to the ethics of care.

REFERENCES

Gilligan, C. (1982). *In a different voice: Psychological theory and women's development*. Cambridge, MA: Harvard University Press.

Gilligan, C. (2011). *Joining the resistance*. Malden, MA: Polity Press.

Gilligan, C., & Richards, D. A. J. (2009). *The deepening darkness: Patriarchy, resistance & democracy's future*. New York, NY: Cambridge University Press.

Gilligan, C., Rogers, A. G., Tolman, D. L. (Eds.) (1991). *Women, girls & psychotherapy: Reframing resistance*. Binghamton, NY: Harrington Park Press.

Goldberg, M. F. (2000). An interview with Carol Gilligan: Restoring lost voices. *Phi Delta Kappan, 81*(9) 701–702, 704.

Gould, K. H. (1988). Old wine in new bottles: A feminist perspective on Gilligan's theory. *Social Work, 33*(5), 411–15.

Meece, J. L. & Daniels, D. H. (2008). *Child & adolescent development for educators* (3rd ed.). New York: McGraw-Hill.

New York University School of Law. (2012). *Carol Gilligan – NYU School of Law-Biography*. Retrieved from https://its.law.nyu.edu/facultyprofiles/profile.cfm?section=bio&personID=19946

Taylor, J. M., Gilligan, C., & Sullivan, A. M. (1997). *Between voice and silence: Women and girls, race and relationship*. Cambridge, MA: Harvard University Press.

MARIKA BARTO & APRIL WHATLEY BEDFORD

16. HENRY GIROUX

Man on Fire

INTRODUCTION

A common belief of social justice educators and critical theorists is that their philosophies of education are grounded in their life histories, and Henry Giroux is an exemplar of that belief. Born in Providence, Rhode Island in 1943, Giroux grew up in poverty in a working class neighborhood, attended college on a basketball scholarship, and taught high school social studies in segregated Baltimore. During his teacher preparation and early teaching career, Giroux discovered the work of Paulo Freire and Howard Zinn and, from that point on, he "was on fire, and fortunately the fire never went out" (Peters, 2011, background and reflection section, paragraph 10).

Giroux earned his doctorate from Carnegie-Mellon University in 1977 and accepted a faculty position in Education at Boston University. His first book on critical pedagogy, *Ideology, Culture, and the Process of Schooling*, was published in 1981, and because he was perceived as having radical views on education, he was initially denied tenure. While that and other experiences shaped his views on education at all levels, he went on to pursue a successful career in academia in increasingly prominent positions at Miami University of Ohio (1983–1992) and Pennsylvania State University (1992 to 2004). Giroux currently holds the position of Global Television Network Chair in English and Cultural Studies at McMaster University in Ontario, Canada and continues to write and speak passionately about his views on teachers, curriculum, and schools (Peters, 2011).

TEACHERS

Giroux argues that the industrialization of education, as well as the attempt by those in power to reduce teaching and learning to a set of procedures, have turned teachers into "semi-robotic" technicians rather than "engaged intellectuals, willing to construct the classroom conditions that provide the knowledge, skills and culture of questioning necessary for students to participate in critical dialogue with the past, question authority, struggle with ongoing relations of power and prepare themselves for what it means to be active and engaged citizens in the interrelated local, national and global public spheres" (Giroux, 2010, paragraph 6). It is no coincidence, in his analysis, that the industrialization of education also accompanies efforts to reduce

James D. Kirylo (Ed.), A Critical Pedagogy of Resistance: 34 Pedagogues We Need to Know, 61–64.

educational expenditures, as well as opportunities, for all children. Rather than being viewed as the most essential component in the learning process, teachers have recently been demoted to deliverers of pre-packaged curricular programs. Too much emphasis on high-stakes testing has limited the teacher's autonomy in the classroom; devalued teaching of critical thinking; forced teachers to ignore their own ideas, opinions and experiences in favor of compliance and continued employment; silenced the discussion of relationships between education and larger societal issues, and discouraged the creation of citizen activists in the classroom.

The above prevalent positioning of teachers stands in stark contrast to Giroux's exaltation of teachers as professional, transformative individuals and public intellectuals whose job is to help students imagine the "radical possibilities" of an educated mind and an educated citizenry (Giroux, 1988). These radical educators imagined by Giroux would integrate critical values and cultural phenomena into pedagogy, as integral members of teams deciding education strategies and content materials for specific classrooms and individual students. They would question the power of language, interrogate the nature of experiences, and reject the "culture of positivism" in which schooling is "a form of social regulation that moves individuals toward destinies that preserve the world as it now is" rather than imagining the possibilities of what it could be (The Freire Project, 2012, mid-paragraph section on culture of positivism). While such progressive educators do exist in the current educational environment they are disturbingly labeled as incompetent and disrespectful when they refuse to implement oppressive curricular models based on standardized assessments (Giroux, 2010).

CURRICULUM

Much of Giroux's work over the past three decades has focused on critical pedagogy. He identifies students' lived experiences as the defining feature with respect to a curriculum that embraces a critical perspective. Unfortunately, the tide of learning experiences, especially for minority and low-income students, has dramatically shifted, so that today's classrooms are steeped in authoritative and compliance curriculum structures, measured by discriminatory testing instruments. These limited assessments are used to empower lawmakers to make sweeping value judgments about student achievement and teacher and school effectiveness, and subsequently serve to reinforce and perpetuate current hegemonic structures and stereotypes. Acquiring "knowledge" has become independent of time and place and independent of the personal impact human beings have on the process; instead, it has become industrialized, proceduralized and free from values (Hudson, 1999).

In contrast to current practice, Giroux believes educators must feel free to explore the hidden curriculum, uncover assumptions, and interrogate culture since education is both embedded in society and influences social practices and mores. Critical pedagogy is vital to maintaining democracy by developing students into engaged citizens who question practices, people and policies, and affirm the value of diverse knowledge and opinions. Rather than being limited by age level or academic discipline, curriculum, in Giroux's view, must negotiate areas of cultural content that transcend classrooms and borders (Giroux, 2001; 2011a).

SCHOOLS

Giroux is certainly not the first educator to observe that elementary and secondary schools, particularly those that serve low-income students of color, have gradually transformed to more closely resemble prisons through zero-tolerance policies, metal detectors, enhanced security and police presence, and closer relationships with the juvenile justice system. Due to the emergence of these practices, the general public has come to view students as different from previous generations – more behaviorally difficult, disrespectful, and prone to violence. Discipline of students, which used to be within the purview of teachers and school administrators has been by assumed police officers and the courts. Such "penal pedagogies" have replaced the already rare existence of critical education (Giroux, 2009).

Not only an emphasis on crime and punishment but also an obsession with measurement and accountability have resulted in the sabotaging of critical education, asserts Giroux. Elementary and secondary schools were once nurturing venues for children but have devolved into factories where students more closely resemble products. Students from working-class families and racial minorities are treated differently from middle and upper class students, as they are presented with procedural, skill-based curriculums, allowed fewer opportunities for critical thinking, and forced to adhere to more compliance-oriented school norms and culture. Politicians and the public have turned their backs on these students, even though political rhetoric consistently claims that school "reforms" are intended to provide better opportunities for all students. However, Giroux critiques most of our recent "reforms" that serve to destabilize and starve the learning environments of students who come from families with fewer resources, shifting taxpayer dollars out of public schools that serve these students and into privatized entities that may or may not serve all students.

Higher education, like K-12 education, is essential to democracy. Higher education, and teacher education in particular, has recently been attacked by corporations, the military, right wing foundations and conservative religious groups. The autonomy of faculty and graduate students has been obliterated, leaving only a factory-type atmosphere focused on producing credentials, and leading to the downsizing of academic labor through the constant decrease in tenured professors and a drastic increase in adjunct faculty, according to Giroux (Giroux, 2011b; Giroux & Giroux, 2004).

Schools are the "crucial sphere" for creating and educating citizen activists. Now is the time, urges Giroux, to reinvest public interest in educational institutions. These institutions must be viewed critically in order to ensure their function to transform society. Faculty and students at all educational levels must be encouraged to think, judge, assume responsibility for learning, have unconditional freedom to question, and absorb knowledge in a critical manner. This is the heart of critical pedagogy (Hudson, 1999).

REFERENCES

The Freire Project. (2012). Henry Giroux. *The Paulo and Nita Freire International Project for Critical Pedagogy.* Retrieved from http://www.freireproject.org/content/henry-giroux.

Giroux, H. A. (1981). *Ideology, culture, and the process of schooling.* Philadelphia: Temple University Press.

Giroux, H. A. (2001). *Theory and resistance in education: Towards a pedagogy for the opposition.* Westport, CT: Bergin and Garvey.

Giroux, H. A., & Giroux, S. S. (2004). *Take back higher education.* Hampshire, England: Palgrave Macmillan.

Giroux, H. A. (2009). *Youth in a suspect society: Democracy or disability?* Hampshire, England: Palgrave Macmillan.

Giroux, H. A. (2010). In defense of public school teachers. *Fightback TCNJ!* Retrieved from http://archive.truthout.org/in-defense-public-school-teachers-a-time-crisis58567.

Giroux, H. A. (2011a). *On critical pedagogy.* New York: Continuum International Publishing.

Giroux, H. A. (2011b). Rejecting academic labor as a subaltern class: Learning from Paulo Freire and the politics of critical pedagogy. *Fast Capitalism.* Retrieved from http://www.uta.edu/huma/agger/fastcapitalism/8_2/Giroux8_2.html.

Giroux, H. A. (1988). *Teachers as intellectuals: Toward a critical pedagogy of learning* Westport, CT: Bergin and Garvey.

Hudson, M. (1999). Education for change: Henry Giroux and transformative critical pedagogy. *Solidarity.* Retrieved from http://www.solidarity-us.org/node/1734.

Peters, M. A. (2011). Henry Giroux on democracy unsettled: From critical pedagogy to the war on youth. *Truthout.* Retrieved from http://truth-out.org/index.php?option=com_k2&view=item&id=2753:henry-giroux-on-democracy-unsettled-from-critical-pedagogy-to-the-war-on-youth.

17. JESÚS "PATO" GÓMEZ

A Pedagogy of Love

> . . . he was too intelligent, too creative, too revolutionary, and too sensitive for the current structures of our universities.
>
> Ramón Flecha (Pato's Friend)

Jesús "Pato" Gómez was intrigued by love. He believed love was a social phenomenon that should be critically analyzed because of its importance in defining our relationships, which determine who we are as individuals. Pato's scholarship was infused with ideas related to love, liberation and social justice. Throughout his life and work, the critical educator demonstrated a deep empathy for people he felt had no voice in society. Early in his career, Pato sought to understand how power affected romantic relationships by studying the science of love in social contexts. Later, he worked with individuals that were oppressed to develop the "communicative methodology of research" (Kincheloe, 2008, p. 90), which gave voice to groups who were often overlooked or ignored. Pato argued that by including diverse voices in dialogue would allow those who particularly found themselves in oppressive circumstances to critically analyze themselves through the lens of cultural intelligence.

Jesús Javier Gómez Alonso, nicknamed Pato (Duck), was born in 1952 in Bilbao, Spain. As a young adult, Pato joined the resistance against Franco's dictatorship and was linked to Spain's anarchist labor union known as the National Confederation of Labour (Fundación Jesús Gómez, 2012). It seemed Pato was destined for emancipatory education and the social justice work that would define his career as a critical pedagogue.

In 1992, after many years as a hospital administrator, Pato became a professor of research methods in education at the University of Barcelona. At the university, Pato worked closely with the Centre for Research on Theories and Practices for Overcoming Inequalities (CREA), which is a social justice vehicle that empowers individuals to take action and implement solutions to socio-political oppression. At CREA, Pato studied gender violence issues and critically examined love in order to develop a theory about how it influenced power in future relationships and whether the social practices surrounding love were liberating or oppressive. Pato's work expanded to include working with oppressed groups, specifically the Roma people

James D. Kirylo (Ed.), A Critical Pedagogy of Resistance: 34 Pedagogues We Need to Know, 65–68.

(gypsies), in Spain who were traditionally ostracized in mainstream European communities and schools.

SCIENCE OF LOVE

In his book, *El amor de la sociedad del riesgo (Love in a High-Risk Society)* (2004), Pato challenged the idea of love that is often presented in fairy tales. He believed love could be dehumanizing and degrading. He confronted traditional notions of love by asking subjects questions that forced them to consider things like attraction and choice. Who is attractive? Why is he or she chosen as a partner? Pato reasoned that such questions led to a more thorough understanding of ourselves and partially determined the outcome of our lives resulting from the romantic relationships we select.

While studying the science of love, Pato worked with adolescents and studied their relationships in order to identify those who exhibited oppressive and violent tendencies toward their partners. His goal was to help his subjects understand the differences between romantic love and love without passion in order to reject relationships that were violent or degrading. Pato felt that social and political forces often led to oppressive relationships that enabled one partner to dominate the other and was frequently associated with gender violence. He wanted to help individuals "develop the political and ideological clarity necessary to distinguish oppressive and subordinating love from love that is psychologically healthy, liberating and affirming of one's own humanity" (Bartolomé, 2008, p. 1). Pato encouraged subjects to work toward relationships that were based on equality and solidarity.

Pato's research on preventive socialization of gender violence and his investigations into the science of love were instrumental for the SAFO Women's Group at CREA to critically analyze the prevention of gender violence. SAFO is named for the Greek poet Sappho and focuses its work on gender studies and curbing gender-based violence through dialogue. Pato maintained that dialogue helped to interpret the thoughts, feelings, and desires of individuals. Puigvert (2008) fittingly puts it this way, "Pato deeply believed in the possibility of eradicating gender violence through people's capacity to change their desires, tastes, preferences and choices and to achieve satisfactory affective and sexual relationships" (p. 2).

CRITICAL COMMUNICATIVE METHODOLOGY

The communicative methodology of research derived from Pato's work with the Roma people in Spain. The Roma people were an underclass throughout Europe and were often discriminated against due to their race, their perceived lack of education and their unwillingness to adopt mainstream behaviors. Pato believed oppressed groups had the capacity to frame their own dialogue and critically analyze themselves and their role in society. Pato felt the subjects themselves had much to contribute to any academic understanding of their own lifeworld, described by Habermas (1985) as the mutual, informal social and cultural practices and attitudes of a group of people.

Because Pato was trained as a methodologist, he began to explore the boundaries of qualitative methodology, critically attempting intersubjective dialogue with the Romas so they could contribute to their own emancipation on an equal level with researchers. Vargas and Gómez (2003) make the insightful point that, "Through the intersubjective dialogue, researchers and participants jointly produce scientific knowledge and participate in the definition of actions that lead to social and educational change" (para. 61). Instead of working detached from the Roma utilizing the traditional researcher/subject relationship, Pato treated them as equals and included them in the critical analysis. He defined dialogue as "the basis of the process of learning, implies not just talking or discussing issues but promoting co-operation, motivation, self-confidence, solidarity, and thus, instrumental learning of any kind" (Gómez, 2002, p. 13). Pato and the Roma people dialogued together for a shared understanding of the lifeworld.

The communicative methodology used by Pato is more formally known as critical communicative methodology (CCM), which requires that subjects be involved in the critical dialogue of their own critical analysis. Pato wrote extensively about the communicative methodology in his last book, *Metodología Comunicativa Crítica* (*Critical Communicative Methodology*) (2006), maintaining that each participant (subject and researcher) contributes something important for social change. Communicative research disavows hierarchies and treats all knowledge contributions equally to allow for shared meaning-making. The subjects being studied have specific unique experiences and knowledge, while researchers have the academic background to contextualize critical analysis. Pato argued that this intersubjectivity exhibited the transformative power of CCM by including all voices in the critical dialogue. He challenged those in opposition who believed that the oppressed or undereducated could not contribute. Pato insisted that the oppressed have cultural intelligence; therefore, they must become part of the critical process. Vargas and Gómez (2003) argued that this type of communicative research methodology is holistic and furthers the cause of social justice because of its egalitarianism.

CONCLUSION

In 2003, doctors diagnosed Pato with lung cancer. The tumors were removed; however, two years later doctors discovered the cancer had spread to Pato's liver. In October 2005, he was given two months to live, but survived for 10 more months before succumbing to the disease. He died on August 8, 2006.

Pato Gómez spent his career challenging the traditional researcher/subject relationship in order to give voice to oppressed peoples. Pato was concerned with changing the sociocultural milieu by establishing equality and arguing for social justice through love and friendship. When he noted that love relationships often resulted in violence, he began seeking alternative paths to resocialization that would foster healthy romantic relationships.

Pato used the critical communicative methodology to include more diverse voices in the dialogue that critically examined those who were underserved or ignored by the mainstream. He concluded that the individuals themselves knew best what social change they had accomplished and what was still necessary to achieve their liberty.

Pato's son, Aito, his wife Lidia, and his lifelong friend Ramón Flecha (founder of CREA), are all academics at universities in Europe. The trio has continued to build on Pato's work surrounding CCM and the prevention of gender violence (Gómez, Puigvert and Flecha, 2011).

REFERENCES

Bartolomé, L. (2008). Authentic cariño and respect in minority education: The political and ideological dimensions of love. *International Journal of Critical Pedagogy, 1*(1).

Flecha, R. (2012). http://www.freireproject.org/content/jesus-pato-gomez-ramon-flecha-and-crea.

Fundación Jesús Gómez. (2012). Biography. http://www.fundacionjesusGómez.org/bio_en.php

Gómez, A., Puigvert, L., & Flecha, R. (2011). Critical communicative methodology: Informing real social transformation through research. *Qualitative Inquiry, 17*(3), 235–245.

Gómez, J. (2004). *El amor de la sociedad del riesgo: Una tentativa educativa*. Barcelona: El Roure.

Gómez, J. (2002). Learning communities: When learning in common means school success for all. *MCT, 20*(2), 13–17.

Gómez, J., Latorre, A., Flecha, R., & Sanchez, M. (2006). *Metodología comunicativa crítica*. Barcelona: El Roure.

Habermas, J. (1985). *The theory of communicative action, volumen 2: Lifeworld and system: A critique of functionalist reason*. Boston: Beacon Press.

Kincheloe, J. (2008). *Critical Pedagogy*. New York: Peter Lang.

Puigvert, L. (2008). Breaking the silence: The struggle against gender violence in universities. *International Journal of Critical Pedagogy, 1*(1).

Vargas, J. & Gómez, J. (2003). Why Roma do not like mainstream schools: Voices of a people without territory. *Harvard Educational Review, 73*(4), 559–590.

ARTURO RODRIGUEZ & MATTHEW DAVID SMITH

18. ANTONIO GRAMSCI

Life and Impact on Critical Pedagogy

EARLY LIFE AND EDUCATION

Antonio Gramsci was born in the province of Cagliarli, Sardinia on 22 January 1891. One of seven children, his formative years was spent roaming the hills of Sardinia. Antonio's political understanding was heavily influenced by the Socialism of his brother Gennaro and the imprisonment of his father, Francesco, from 1898–1904. Francesco's imprisonment caused Antonio to curtail his formal education and take up employment. This continued for several years until Francesco was released, allowing young Antonio to return to formal studies.

In the ensuing years Gennaro, with his introduction to socialist literature, was largely responsible for Antonio's political education and for igniting his hunger for knowledge (Rosengarten, 2012). Throughout the period preceding his university studies, Antonio bore witness to social unrest and military repression across Sardinia, swaying him to the cause of Sardinian nationalism efforts (Gramsci, 1971a). Antonio, however, quickly ended his nationalistic tendencies and refocused his attention to the international working-class movement.

In 1911 Gramsci earned a scholarship to the University of Turin where he showed great promise in linguistics and philosophy, delving into the writings of Hegel, Marx, and Engels. However, due to recurring health challenges and difficult learning environments, Gramsci was forced to leave the university before the conclusion of his studies only to find himself sustaining his intellectual curiosities through journalism by writing articles and position papers for leftist newspapers. At the time, the social climate of Turin was one of transition and industrialization; with a population boom and the growth of companies such as Fiat, it was then Gramsci began to take part in organizing trade unions and advocate for the enactment of workers' councils.

Gramsci eventually joined the *Partito Comunista d'Italia* (PCI), and while visiting Russia in 1922, it enabled him to gain much insight of the fascism that was unfolding in Italy. In 1923 Mussolini arrested the general leadership of the PCI, leaving Gramsci in charge. In 1926, with the enactment of fascist laws and Mussolini's purge of political dissidents, Gramsci was placed under arrest and sentenced to prison. His health declined throughout his imprisonment, and following several prison transfers, solitary confinement, and malnutrition he was discharged from prison for hospital stays. While in a hospital in Rome, Gramsci passed away in

James D. Kirylo (Ed.), A Critical Pedagogy of Resistance: 34 Pedagogues We Need to Know, 69–72.

1937 at the age of 46. Yet it was during his time in prison, Gramsci composed over 3,000 pages on history, philosophy, and political economy. His work has inspired a number of past and contemporary critical theorists, critical pedagogues, political economists, and Marxists, among others.

A BRIEF REVIEW OF CENTRAL THOUGHTS IN GRAMSCI'S *SELECTIONS FROM THE PRISON NOTEBOOKS*

Across the 30 notebooks, Gramsci wrote throughout his incarceration, he covered a range of topics and themes revealing that his early termination of university studies did not hinder his learning. To that end, as outlined in Gramsci's *Selections from the Prison Notebooks* (1971b), the following explores a few of the central tenets of Gramsci's thought.

The Two Types of Intellectuals – Gramsci distinguishes between two categories of intellectual: the traditional and the organic. The traditional intellectual is trained/taught within a specific academic field and his/her operations are conducted from a position of concealment/disregard for social class. That is, traditional intellectuals, by and large, lack a concrete or critically conscious connection to a subject of inquiry that might relate the subject ecologically. The organic intellectual concretizes their understandings as he/she enacts their membership in a group. Gramsci (1971b) writes that, "organic intellectuals are distinguished less by their profession...than by their function in directing the ideas and aspirations of the class to which they organically belong" (p. 3). An organic intellectual is thus ecologically related to the social and material experience of human beings. The above binary separation of intellectuals permeates a multitude of topics in the *Prison Notebooks*.

Cultural Hegemony – Perhaps the most well-known of Gramsci's philosophy is his notion of cultural hegemony. Gramsci explains that the method in which a capitalist state maintains control, power over its citizens, is through the dominance of cultural aspects, processes, and norms. As a result, the ideology of the dominant class comes to be subtly and overtly accepted by the subordinate classes who in turn normalize an ideology through their daily engagement and practice. As a process of intellectual and practical dominance, the subordinated groups internalize the dominant class's ideology and though it be counter to their own best interests the dominated classes may succumb to its logic.

War of Position and War of Maneuver – For Gramsci, two distinct options were at the disposal of subordinated classes in the midst of class struggle: war of position and war of maneuver. The war of position is conducted whereby the oppressed classes and organic intellectuals plan, organize, and enact a reality that actively opposes the imposed norms and counteracts the cultural hegemony of the ruling class. The war of maneuver is thus the physical overcoming and deposing of the ruling class. Consequently, it is necessary that the war of position precede the war of manoeuvre.

Education – Gramsci's writing on education can be seen as a direct precursor to those scholars that investigate concepts related to the sociology of education,

education and social class, the debate of instruction versus education, and ideology and education. For Gramsci (1971b), relationships must be drawn between the school and the lived experiences of the students, asserting "the individual consciousness of the overwhelming majority of children reflects social and cultural relations which are different from and antagonistic to those which are represented in the school curricula..." (p. 35). Thus, one can particularly see the influence of Gramsci on the thinking that frames critical pedagogy, particular with respect to examining the incongruence of the lived experiences of children and the official school curriculum. His critique of the disconnection between schooling and society compels us to consider the motives of those responsible for producing and sanctioning "official" curricula.

CONNECTION TO CRITICAL PEDAGOGY

To say Gramsci's legacy influences education is stating the matter lightly. Indeed, his thinking continues to be relevant across the critical tradition; the following are just a few notable examples:

Paulo Freire-Organic/Academic Intellectual – Gramsci and Freire clearly share common intellectual interests which include, among others, Hegel, Marx, and Engels. Freire's discussion of the revolutionary educator (Freire, 2003) as an agent in overcoming both the banking method of education (which only serves to reproduce a dominant ideology) and the teacher-student binary (central to banking education and frequently upheld by the Academic Intellectual) is congruent with Gramsci's notion of the Organic Intellectual, an anchor in critical pedagogy.

Henry A. Giroux-Education – In his analysis of the role and purpose of public education today, Giroux draws from Gramsci to illustrate the reinforcement of dominant ideology embedded both in public education and beyond the classroom (public pedagogy). To fully grasp how the dominant group shapes public education and social media, it is necessary to first understand what is directly at stake (Giroux, 2001). Much of Gramsci's descriptions of ideology then resonate with critical pedagogy by providing analytical tools for educators, students, and social activists to interrogate and challenge those dominant modes.

Peter McLaren-War of Position and War of Maneuver – For Peter McLaren, Gramsci's war of position and war of maneuver are central to the political and economic world in which we are currently situated. McLaren (2007) asserts that "we are currently living in... a 'war of position'" (p. 313) in that we are presently engaged in unifying a diverse network of socially and politically active networks; this will allow an opportunity for a war of maneuver. For critical pedagogues, the classroom is a site for a war of position.

Donaldo Macedo-Cultural Hegemony – For years, Donaldo Macedo has challenged oppressive linguistic policies and practices. Recognizing that questions of language are veneers directly related to power and control, Macedo's resistance and challenge to linguistic oppression articulates a similar position to Gramsci's theory of cultural hegemony. Policies that restrict or officialize one language (particularly in educational settings) are tools for dis-abling language minority populations. This oppression extends far beyond the classroom; over time, languages other than English are killed, with them the inherent logic and systems of thought that exist among their speakers (Macedo, 2006).

CONCLUSION

Revolutions do not occur spontaneously. They are the work of individuals who engage the human and not so human experiences they encounter and then dream ways to transform them. Antonio Gramsci's work clearly influences the struggle over the commodification of human beings, building a more humanized reality. He understood as Freire, Giroux, McLaren and Macedo reflect, if we consider their life's work, the human experience is one we are more fully born into as we engage experience and consider our relationships with the world and each other.

REFERENCES

Boggs, C. (1976). *Gramsci's Marxism.* Camelot Press Limited: Southampton, UK.

Boggs, C. (1984). *The two revolutions: Antonio Gramsci and the dilemmas of western Marxism.* Boston, MA: South End Press.

Freire, P. (2003). *Pedagogy of the oppressed.* Continuum: New York.

Giroux, H. A. (2001). *Theory and resistance in education: Towards a pedagogy for the opposition.* Westport, CT: Bergin & Garvey.

Gramsci, A. (1971a). *Men of flesh and blood.* L'Ordine Nuovo. Retrieved from: www.marxists.org/archive/gramsci/

Gramsci, A. (1971b). *Selections from the prison notebooks.* Q. Hoare & G. Nowell Smith, (Eds.). New York, NY: International Publishers.

Joll, J. (1977). *Gramsci.* Glasgow, Scotland: William Collins Sons and Co.

Macedo, D. (2006). *Literacies of power: What Americans are not allowed to know.* Boulder, CO: Westview Press.

McLaren, P. (2007). *Life in schools: An introduction to critical pedagogy in the foundations of education.* (5th ed.). Allyn & Bacon: Boston.

Rosengarten, F. (2012). *An introduction to Gramsci's life and thought.* Retrieved from: www.marxists.org/archive/gramsci/

DEBORA BASLER WISNESKI

19. BELL HOOKS

Scholar, Cultural Critic, Feminist, and Teacher

BIRTH OF A WRITER AND TEACHER

bell hooks has been given many titles throughout her career- social activist, feminist, intellectual, poet, author, cultural critic, academic and most importantly, particularly for those in the field of education, teacher. She was born on September 25, 1952 as Gloria Jean Watkins in Hopkinsville, Kentucky. As one of six children, the daughter of a custodian and housewife, she loved to read and recite poetry. Growing up in the segregated south, her early schooling experiences were positive as she was mentored by supportive black teachers; however, it was during the time that she entered an integrated high school that her awareness level was heightened as she came face to face with racist white teachers who viewed her and her black classmates as inferior and incapable of learning. Despite the challenges and obstacles that could have easily thwarted her from entering the university and pursuing her dreams to be a writer, hooks went on to graduate from Stanford with a degree in English, later a master's in English at the University of Wisconsin-Madison, and a doctorate in literature from the University of California, Santa Cruz. (Burke, 2004; hooks, 1994)

Her first work *And There We Wept: Poems* was published in 1978 under her pen name bell hooks. She chose the name bell hooks to honor her mother and grandmother's names and to distance herself and her work from her identity as Gloria Watkins. She uses lower case in her name to emphasize her work rather than her identity. Her most notable publication, *Ain't I A Woman? Black Women and Feminism,* came later in 1981, although she had written the manuscript at age 19 while still in college. This text drew attention to her as an influential voice in feminist thought. Since then, hooks has gone on to write over 30 books in the form of critical essays, poetry, and children's literature and multiple articles for professional and popular journals in the field of cultural criticism and theory, education, literature, and feminist theory. Her texts cover a range of explorations related to race, gender, class, culture, and sexuality. Simultaneously while she has been immersed in her writing, she also has taught at the university level. Her academic career began at the University of California, Santa Cruz, then onto Yale University, Oberlin College, City College of New York, and currently at Berea College in Kentucky. While hooks longed to be a writer and only taught as a way to support her writing, she pleasantly

James D. Kirylo (Ed.), A Critical Pedagogy of Resistance: 34 Pedagogues We Need to Know, 73–76.

discovered great personal joy and passion in teaching (Adams, 2005; Burke, 2004; hooks, 1994).

FROM THE MARGINS

hooks has identified herself as living on the margins of society which means "being a part of the whole but outside the main body" (hooks, 2000c, p. xvi.) and, thus, has been able to provide a perspective to education that challenges the status quo. Her critical perspective draws widely across many fields and she weaves together the ideas of such leaders as the Brazilian educator Paulo Freire, abolitionist and feminist Sojourner Truth, civil rights leader Martin Luther King, Jr., and the Buddhist teachings of Pema Chodron and Thich Nhat Hanh. Her essays are often written in a postmodern way that allows the reader to grapple with dense cross-disciplinary theories, connect to personal stories, and feel as if one is having a conversation with hooks and her influences simultaneously.

While her writing is gentle and clear, her ideas strongly challenge and confront oppression and injustice at many levels. For example, in her texts on feminism hooks simply clarifies and simplifies feminist theory as "a movement to end sexism, sexist exploitation, and oppression" (hooks, 2000a, p. 1), yet she delves into the history of feminist movements and challenges the limitations of speaking against sexism without acknowledging the complexities it brings with race, class, and ethnicity. hooks also reminds her readers, particularly feminists, that part of the process of fighting sexism is to confront the sexism women have internalized and the patriarchal ways they may actually think and act. Here, hooks' perspective illuminates how even feminist theory that strives for equity can marginalize others. Another example of hooks' ability to confront oppression from the margins is through her exploration of classism and critical theory that attempts to address economic injustices, arguing that discussions of class are often substantively lacking and generally limited to the perspectives of white privileged males. She underscores the importance of highlighting the voices and personal experiences of the working class and poor across racial and gender lines and recognizes that these perspectives provide us with the potential to build community. As she suggests, the struggle for economic social justice can unite "groups that have never before taken a stand together to support their common hope of living in a more democratic and just world" (hooks, 2000b, p. 120). Thus, her view from the margins of society provides educators an example of addressing injustices by valuing the voices of the "other" while working simultaneously to find spaces for togetherness.

In an effort to fight oppression and make the case of what it means to move toward self-actualization and live freely in a democratic community, hooks impressively explores pedagogy, teaching, and learning in a trilogy of texts on education: *Teaching to Transgress: Education as a Practice of Freedom* (1994); *Teaching Community: A Pedagogy of Hope* (2003); and, *Teaching Critical Thinking: Practical Wisdom* (2010).

In *Teaching to Transgress*, hooks asserts that the institutional boundaries that are established in classrooms are generally from a patriarchal white supremacist perspective that fosters a banking approach to learning which ignores the presence and experiences of the students and even the teacher. In response, hooks suggests that American schools should develop classroom communities that cultivate engagement in authentic learning and whose purpose is to "transgress" the boundaries that keep a diverse student population from becoming self-actualized. Her form of "engaged pedagogy" is a blend of critical pedagogies, inspired by Freire's notion of conscientization, and enhanced by the Buddhist teachings of Thich Nhat Hanh which views teaching as a healing practice. That is, teaching and learning is a holistic experience that takes a radical approach of allowing students opportunities to share their stories, listen to the voices of others, and enter into difficult discussions to create a shared knowledge that uplifts the participants. In *Teaching Community* she calls on educators to teach democratically in such a way that action moves beyond the classroom, actively working in the community to end racism and oppressive structures. Her text *Teaching Critical Thinking* challenges educators to approach teaching as an art form, a vocation, and an exercise of free speech for all. Ultimately, an engaged pedagogy is a process of building relationships with others based on respect and equality in order to build a democratic society free from oppression.

A VISION OF LOVE

Just as educators will find deep meaning in hooks' cultural critiques and her call for a more liberatory approach to education, her essays on love offer much to us, as well. Exploring how we struggle with defining love, how we demonstrate love in action, and how children learn about love, all within a world that can be harsh and oppressive, hooks provides insight and wisdom summed in the simple, but profound notion that "Love is as love does..." (hooks, 2001, p. 30). Particularly with respect to children, hooks challenges adults to recognize that children are not property, have rights, and are in need of adults who respect those rights. Moreover, hooks maintains that while love is necessarily realized in self, in romance, friendships, and families, it is often best manifested as a collective community affair. In the end, guided by the profound virtue of love, bell hooks is a champion toward ending racism, sexism, inequalities, and discrimination, and creating a more just world.

REFERENCES

Adams, M. (2005). bell hooks Creates Community at Berea. Retrieved from http://www.berea.edu/bcnow-archive/story.asp?ArticleID=474.
Burke, B. (2004). 'Bell Hooks on education'. *The encyclopedia of informal education.* Retrieved from www.infed.org/thinkers/hooks.htm.
hooks, b. (1978). *And there we wept: poems.* Los Angeles, CA: Golemics.
hooks, b. (1981). *Ain't I a woman?: Black women and feminism.* Cambridge, MA: South End Press.
hooks, b. (1994). *Teaching to transgress: Education as the practice of freedom.* New York, NY: Routledge.
hooks, b. (2000a). *Feminism is for everybody: Passionate politics.* Cambridge, MA: South End Press.

hooks, b. (2000b). *Where we stand: Class matters.* New York, NY: Routledge.

hooks, b. (2000c). *Feminist theory: From margin to center.* (2nd Ed.). Cambridge, MA: South End Press.

hooks, b. (2001). *All about love: New visions.* New York, NY: Harper Perennial.

hooks, b. (2003). *Teaching community: A pedagogy of hope.* New York, NY: Routledge.

hooks, b. (2010). *Teaching critical thinking: Practical wisdom.* New York, NY: Routledge.

TONDRA L. LODER-JACKSON

20. MYLES HORTON

The Critical Relevance of his Work in the 21st Century

There are only about a half dozen books published exclusively on the life and work of Myles Horton. Countless more, however, include entries on and references to Horton's profound influence on 20th century democracy and education in the U.S. Yet there is still more that could and should be published about Horton's legacy, particularly its transcendence into 21st century American education and society. This chapter covers ground traversed by previous biographers, including Horton himself. But perhaps more so than in previous works, this chapter links Horton's legacy to modern-day challenges, problems, and promises inherent in mobilizing education as a vehicle for social change, particularly in university teacher education and educational leadership programs. This modern-day application is framed from the perspective of Horton's "two-eyed" approach – where with one eye he looked at people as they were, while with the other he looked at what they might become (Horton, J. Kohl, & H. R. Kohl, 1998, p. 33).

BIOGRAPHICAL SKETCH

Myles Horton's White Southern working class roots unquestionably inform his life and legacy as a social activist, educator, and thinker. He was born on July 9, 1905 in Savannah, Tennessee to two school teachers, Elsie Falls Horton and Perry Horton. Both parents lost their jobs when teaching requirements were expanded to include one year of high school, which exceeded their formal education. After Horton's birth followed three siblings, brothers Delmas and Daniel, and sister, Elsie Pearl. After losing their jobs as teachers, the Hortons earned a living through various low-skilled jobs. Horton's parents were socially conscious and civic-minded as noted by his father's participation in the Worker's Alliance, a union of the Worker's Progress Administration (WPA), and his mother's self-initiated neighborhood literacy programs. Raised in the Cumberland Presbyterian Church, Horton credited his parents for teaching him about the virtues of service, education, and being a Christian neighbor.

In pursuit of education beyond elementary school Horton was compelled to leave home at age 15 to attend high school in Forkadeer River Valley, Tennessee. His parents followed him there at great economic sacrifice, but Horton opted to continue living independently and working odd jobs in saw mills and factories since his

James D. Kirylo (Ed.), A Critical Pedagogy of Resistance: 34 Pedagogues We Need to Know, 77–80.
© *2013 Sense Publishers. All rights reserved.*

father was unemployed at the time. As a high school student, he embarked upon his first "union" leadership role at a crate-making job, where he convinced other youth laborers to stop working after their demands for a raise were initially rejected by the owners. Their temporary work stoppage and irreplaceable work acumen forced the owners to rehire them with increased pay.

In 1924 Horton's church encouraged him to attend Cumberland University in Lebanon, Tennessee. He recalled that the library compensated for the lack of "good teachers" (Horton as cited in Jacobs, 2003, p. 145). One of those good teachers was a newly-minted sociology professor and alumnus of the University of Chicago, who reinforced Horton's interest in unions. Horton also played football and participated in a racially-tolerant Student YMCA. But Horton eventually rejected the Student YMCA's accommodationist practice of publicly adhering to segregation laws while privately espousing integration. His view was that "you learn what you do, and not what you talk about" (Horton, J. Kohl, & H. R. Kohl, 1998, p. 16). In 1928 he put his convictions into practice as secretary of the state branch of the Student YMCA, where one of his boldest moves – clandestinely organizing 120 statewide student officers for its first interracial banquet – set the stage for his subsequent involvement in the 1950s and 1960s civil rights movement.

EDUCATION FOR SOCIAL CHANGE

After college Horton attended the University of Chicago and Union Theological Seminary in New York City. He was influenced by several prominent people who, over time, became more like comrades than mentors. Some of them included theologian Reinhold Niebuhr, progressive philosophers John Dewey and Jane Addams, and social reconstructionist, George Counts. Horton also learned from famous activists who graced the campus of the legendary Highlander School, which was co-founded in 1932 in Monteagle, Tennessee by him, Don West, and James A. Dombrowki. Some of these activists included Eleanor Roosevelt, Reverend Dr. Martin Luther King, Rosa Parks, Mississippi voting rights activist Fannie Lou Hamer, and South Carolina teacher-activist, Septima Clark. Notably, Horton and Brazilian educational philosopher and activist, Paulo Freire, shared a mutual affinity and respect for each other's worldviews and contributions. Horton met his wife, the former Zilphia Johnson, in 1935 when she was a student in Highlander's labor union workshop. She is credited with linking the cultural arts, most notably folk music, to Highlander's activist curriculum (Carter, 1994).

Seeds for the Highlander School idea were sown during Horton's brief matriculation at the University of Chicago where he learned about the Danish Folk School movement, a grassroots education experiment that emerged from community members' frustration with the disengagement of Denmark schooling. Danish folk schools sought to engage students more intimately by challenging them to propose, analyze, and solve important life questions and problems. Horton visited Denmark to witness these schools for himself and returned to the U.S. ready to launch a new vision for adult education that would create a new social order. Horton's adult education pedagogy was grassroots, proactive, community-relevant, and egalitarian. He believed that the ultimate purpose of education was to change the world for the better. Teachers and students shared equal status in classroom and on campus. All were assigned chores as agreed upon in their communal space. They were all responsible for co-constructing a meaningful and relevant teaching and learning environment.

Highlander was an incomparable intellectual foundation for 20th century labor rights (1930s through early 1940s) and civil rights movements (1940s through early 1960s). However, in the mid-1950s and 1960s Highlander faced mounting attacks from White Southern segregationists. Tennessee officials revoked Highlander's charter and confiscated its property after the school was rocked by mounting legislative investigations, damning propaganda campaigns, and high-profile legal trials. On October 9, 1961, after the U.S. Supreme Court refused to review a Tennessee Supreme Court decision upholding Highlander's charter revocation order, Highlander was officially closed. However, in 1962 Highlander was revived as the Highlander Research and Education Center (HREC) in Knoxville, Tennessee. Regrettably, Highlander never regained the stature and influence it once had on 20th century American social consciousness.

HORTON'S LEGACY IN 21ST CENTURY AMERICAN EDUCATION

The demise of the original Highlander School has left a chasm in American democracy and education. Where is today's major democratic think tank for educators, community leaders, and activists? Sadly, old-guard civil rights and labor rights organizations that have stood the test of time have suffered Highlander's fate of falling into relative obscurity and irrelevancy. Should today's educational institutions, namely those university teacher educator and educational leadership programs responsible for preparing successive generations of educators, be challenged to revisit and revive the legacy of Horton and Highlander? No doubt, very few university programs are even remotely familiar with Myles Horton and the Highlander School. A case in point is the recent trend in K-12 schools to create *professional learning communities* (PLCs), where educators learn what works best in their schools primarily from each other rather than from external actors such as education reformers, bureaucrats, and politicians (R. DuFour, Eaker, & R. DuFour, 2008). Surely Horton's adult education model, emphasizing mutual education, where "friends educate each other," (Horton as cited in Jacobs, 2003, p. 211), collaborative problem-solving, intergenerational capacity-building, and democratic values are essential to creating authentic PLCs. Yet, unfortunately, Horton's tried-and-true pedagogy is seldom if ever acknowledged in PLC literature.

Perhaps Horton's obscurity in traditional university teacher education and educational leadership programs may be explained by Horton himself. He asked: "What role should schools serve in building or reconstructing a society?" (Horton as cited in Jacobs, 2003, p. 228). For Horton, the answer lay with the kind of society citizens aspired to achieve. His concern was that schools are bound by the economic system in which they are situated. In response, he believed it would take a people's movement to liberate education, and eventually, society. If schools are to change, then educators must reach out to people beyond the four walls of the school to exchange ideas. Horton called for teachers to "stop talking primarily to each other" and come out of their comfort zones and collaborate to build a people's movement to democratize schooling (Horton as cited in Jacobs, 2003, p. 229). To this I would add that when educators talk to each other, they should reevaluate their dialogue and actions. How might they band together to create better schools and societies rather than react in passive dissent to educational reforms and policies that external actors impose upon them? Furthermore, in those instances when educators take bold and public stands to protect their professional standing, how might they also vocalize their concern and commitment to issues (e.g., inequitable school funding) directly relevant to those whom they serve? In light of increasing cultural and family diversity, how might educators bridge gaps that potentially alienate them from students and families? Perhaps the conceptualization and implementation of PLCs could be rethought and expanded to include students, parents, and community members in some meaningful way. Horton's posthumous challenge for American educators in the 21st century is for us to join ranks with surrounding communities, taking into consideration their unique local color and associated problems and potential, to reconstruct a more educated, just, and humane society.

REFERENCES

Adams, F. (1975). *Unearthing seeds of fire: The idea of Highlander*. Charlotte, NC: Heritage.

Ayers, B. & Quinn, T. (n.d.). Myles Horton (1905–1990). *Education encyclopedia State University.com*. Retrieved from: http://education.stateuniversity.com/pages/2072/Horton-Myles-1905 –1990.html

Bell, B., Gaventa, J., & Peters, J. (1990). *We make the road by walking: Conversations on education and social change/Myles Horton and Paulo Freire*. Philadelphia, PA: Temple University Press.

Carter, V. K. (1994, Spring). The singing heart of Highlander Folk School. *New Horizons in Adult Education, 8*(2), 4–24.

Dufour, R., Eaker, R., & Dufour, R. (2008). *Revisiting professional learning communities at work: New insights for improving schools*. Bloomington, IN: Solution Tree.

Glen, J. M. (1988). *Highlander: No ordinary school 1932–1962*. Lexington, KY: University Press of Kentucky.

Horton, M., Kohl, J., & Kohl, H. R. (1998). *The long haul: An autobiography*. New York City, NY: Teachers College Press.

Jacobs, D. (Ed.). (2003). *The Myles Horton reader: Education for social change*. Knoxville, TN: The University of Tennessee Press.

DEBRA PANIZZON

21. IVAN ILLICH

Renegade Academic, Intellectual, and Pastor

A critical pedagogist, Ivan Illich (1926–2002) was concerned with the ways in which education as provided by schooling perpetuated and even legitimized social injustice and inequity. In 1971, Illich published one of his most famous books, *Deschooling Society*. Considered radical and extremely revolutionary at the time, it called for the disestablishment of schools (i.e., from early childhood through to university) as the chief mandating institutions for the process of education. Illich's concern was that *institutionalized* education merely prepared individuals for specific vocations within the burgeoning industrialized economy of the 1960–70s, not for a meaningful life. The production-line processes, hierarchical and rigid structures, and explicit itemized curricula that comprised schooling at the time aimed to create dependent moulded citizens for an employment niche within industrialized society (Illich, 1973). Critically, he was not opposed to learning and understanding but considered that the education provided by schooling devalued cultural and individual differences creating greater class division and social inequity (Illich, 1971).

With epistemological views aligned most closely to Marxist philosophies, knowledge for Illich was a "function of active engagement in real situations" (Bowen & Hobson, 1987, p. 391). This conception of education was embedded around a village model of existence whereby everyday activities were learning opportunities that benefitted not just the individual but also the social collective. Learning did not require a certified teacher but was the product of an individual's curiosity, alertness, and engagement in a range of activities and interactions with others in the community. Not surprisingly, this view conflicted with what Illich observed globally where the formalization of education within schools and universities resulted in the compartmentalization of knowledge into packages (termed *commodities*) for dissemination to students at specified times often culminating in knowledge that was meaningless and irrelevant to the learner. As such this knowledge benefitted neither the individual nor society.

At the crux of the deschooling issue for Illich was the hidden curriculum, which ensured that while individuals completed a legislated number of years of schooling, they were also enculturated into societal norms and ideologies that perpetuated traditional class structures and inequity (Illich & Verne, 1976). The implication of this enculturation suggests that the only knowledge that comes from formal schooling

James D. Kirylo (Ed.), A Critical Pedagogy of Resistance: 34 Pedagogues We Need to Know, 81–84.
© *2013 Sense Publishers. All rights reserved.*

would ensure future prosperity (i.e., schooling led to wealth). In other words, using subversive and almost indoctrinating means, schools created a dependency upon school knowledge so that "permanent education beco[a]me not the symbol of our unfinished development, but a guarantee of our permanent inadequacy" (Illich & Verne, 1976, p. 13). Even in 1976, Illich predicted that acceptance of this view would create an expectation that the entire life of individuals might be locked into schooling. Within such a culture, schools and universities become self-perpetuating institutions with the consumers of knowledge enjoying higher income, social status and other privileges evident in all industrialized societies, contrasting greatly to the expectations of individuals in poorer less developed nations (Pauly, 1983). Hence, for Illich, schools occupied a powerful position polarizing and controlling society by determining who was educated, what knowledge was taught, when this knowledge was made available in the curriculum, and equally important, which societal values were supported and reinforced by the schooling system.

Philosophically, Illich considered schools and universities to be unbalanced institutions on a par with the army, penitentiaries, and even monasteries in that all comprised sub-populations of society that needed to be managed by formalized procedures and rigorous discipline. Clearly, the advantage of these methods was that individuals were pressured to conform resulting in a high degree of societal control or *manipulation*. This was hugely problematic for Illich not just in principle but also because of the funds allocated toward the development of strategies to maintain this control (i.e., funding research in psychology and sociology in relation to issues around student disengagement with schooling) (Bowen & Hobson, 1987).

While the focus here is schooling and education, Illich questioned the legitimacy of all industrial institutions including the legal, media, medical, and transport systems along with the Catholic Church. For example, in his book *Medical Nemisis* (1975), Illich argued that medicalization caused greater harm than good creating individuals that were dependent on medical services resulting in many lifelong patients. At the time of publication his views had little impact in the medical arena but some 27 years later, many of his attitudes and views have been adopted creating massive changes to health care, particularly in relation to doctor-patient relationships (Wright, 2003).

Illich has been described as a renegade academic, intellectual, and pastor in the literature. All these descriptions are based in truth in that he was extremely well educated having studied histology and crystallography at the University of Florence, theology and philosophy at the Pontifical Gregorian University in the Vatican, and completed a doctorate in sociology at Harvard University. Furthermore, he was an ordained Catholic priest and spent many years working with Puerto Rican immigrants in New York City and later in Puerto Rico and Mexico (Kahn & Kellner, 2007). However, so vehement were his criticisms of the institutionalized church that he was forced to renounce his rights as a priest losing the title of Monsignor.

Given Illich's own educational background, there is a degree of irony here: *Could Illich have challenged and questioned so vociferously in the public arena without the very schooling he abhorred?* It might be argued that it was this breadth and depth of understanding across a range of fields (e.g., science, religion, sociology, languages) along with his ability to "link politics and culture, capitalist economics and human ethics to a rigorous critique of schooling" (Kahn & Kellner, 2007, p. 431) that made Illich a most credible adversary for the social institutions of the time! But how relevant are these somewhat radical and extremist views in relation to 21st century education? By stepping back from the detail, it is possible to identify a number of issues around schooling predicted by Illich that are prevalent today. For example:

- Many highly industrialized countries currently have a pool of university graduates that cannot find employment appropriate to their level of schooling. The result is that they are either encouraged to move onto the next degree or find alternative employment outside of their field of expertise. Unfortunately, this is also the case for students with a Doctorate of Philosophy (PhD).
- Schools and universities have increasingly become financial institutions with students considered as *clients* paying for their 'compartmentalized packages of knowledge'. With this payment comes the expectation of success, resulting in a higher degree of scrutiny and accountability on teaching with seemingly less focus on the responsibilities of students as learners.
- In my own area of specialization, there are global issues around the engagement of students in science and mathematics careers with considerable research literature alluding to the importance of teaching these subjects contextually so that that they are meaningful and relevant to students. Linked to this is the importance of informal learning experiences, such as interactions with scientists, engineers or members of the community, along with the opportunities to visit local industries (e.g., wind farms, production of medical devices) where students gain an appreciation of the real-world applications of science in the workplace. All of these pedagogies align closely to Illich's view of *community* learning so that it is both useful and meaningful.
- In terms of funding allocation, many of the large-scale reform agendas in education in a number of highly industrialized countries over the last decade (e.g., *No Child Left Behind* policy in the USA, *Closing the Gap* in Australia) have resulted in minimal impact on improving educational outcomes (literacy and numeracy) and social equity. As alluded to by Illich, the difficulty with many of these policies is that issues of literacy and numeracy (as examples) go beyond the schooling system so they need to be tackled on a number of fronts simultaneously.

So, while perceived a maverick by many, Illich must be considered in the context of his time (1960s-70s) with prevailing concerns around capitalism, globalization, and the move toward large-scale bureaucracy. In this climate, Illich perceived that schooling was focused on compliance and conformity with little regard for individual needs or sensitivities around cultural diversity. Although perhaps extreme in his thinking, by critiquing and challenging the purpose and nature of schooling, Illich paved the way for many of our schools that endeavour to provide socially relevant knowledge to a diverse array of students in ways that are more attentive to their needs and the broader communities in which the schools reside (Gajardo, 2000).

REFERENCES

Bowen, J. & Hobson, P. R. (1987). *Theories of education: Studies of significant innovation in western* education thought. (2nd ed). Brisbane, Australia: Watson Ferguson & Company.

Gajardo, M. (2000). Ivan Illich. *Prospects: The Quarterly Review of Comparative Education, 23*(3–4), 711–720.

Illich, I. (1971). *Deschooling society.* New York: Harper & Row.

Illich, I. (1973). The deschooled society. In P. Buckman, *Education without schools* (pp. 9–19). London: Willmer Brothers Limited.

Illich, I. (1975). *Medical nemesis: The expropriation of health.* London: Marion Boyars Publishers Ltd.

Illich, I. & Verne, E. (1976). *Imprisoned in the global classroom.* London: Writers and Readers Publishing Cooperative.

Kahn, R. & Kellner, D. (2007). Paulo Freire and Ivan Illich: Technology, politics and the reconstruction of education. *Policy Futures in Education, 5*(4), 431–448.

Pauly, J. J. (1983). Ivan Illich and mass communication studies. *Communication Research, 10,* 259–280.

Wright, P. (2003). Obituary: Ivan Illich. *The Lancet, 361*(9352), 185. Retrieved 8th February 2012, from http://www.thelancet.com/journals/lancet/article/PIIS0140–6736(03)12233–7/fulltext.

JOHN C. FISCHETTI & BETTY T. DLAMINI

22. JOE L. KINCHELOE

With Liberty and Justice for All

Joe (Jodie) Lyons Kincheloe, Jr. personified the notion of what it means to live a life that cultivates the concept of "liberty and justice for all." With a laser focus on social justice values, Kincheloe was a critical pedagogue's critical pedagogue, a seminal provocateur reminding us that, while individual educators have the opportunity to make liberty and justice more likely, they need to be critically aware of institutional injustice, as can happen with schools with the perpetuation of inequities and the promotion of maintaining the "haves" and "have-nots" in our society.

Kincheloe is the author/co-author/editor/co-editor of more than 50 books, numerous book-chapters, and hundreds of journal articles on issues related to critical pedagogy, educational research, urban studies, cognition, curriculum, and cultural studies. His vision for the potential of education is insightfully underscored around key challenges he raised about the role of teachers as disseminators of predetermined knowledge of dominant cultural power versus liberators of human potential. "Is teacher education merely the process of developing the most efficient ways for educators to perform this task? Do teachers operate as functionaries who simply do what they are told?" Kincheloe unmasked the hidden curriculum noting that "democracy and justice cannot be separated from teaching and learning" (Kincheloe, 2008a, p. 5).

BIOGRAPHY

Born in 1950 in Kingsport, Tennessee, Kincheloe, an only child of older parents, was intrinsically motivated from his earliest years. His father, Joe Sr., a rural school principal, and his mother, Libby Bird, a third grade teacher, brought him up to oppose the predominant rural Tennessee culture of classism, segregation and racism. Until his own rebellion at about age 12, Kincheloe was immersed in a strong Christian environment that was predominantly led by his uncle Marvin Kincheloe, a Methodist circuit preacher. Kincheloe taught himself to play the piano and became a song writer at a young age, prolifically writing nearly 600 songs throughout the course of his life. Of the transcendent power of music and particularly for his life-long love of rock and roll and the blues, Kincheloe revealed, "Growing up among grotesque forms of classism and racism in the South of the 1950s and 1960s, I soon

James D. Kirylo (Ed.), A Critical Pedagogy of Resistance: 34 Pedagogues We Need to Know, 85–88.

found a means, while still in high school, to bring people together and move them as a blues musician and songwriter" (Steinberg, 2009, p. 1).

An underachiever in the eyes of many of his grade school teachers, Kincheloe was often in disagreement with elders because of his intense dislike for segregation and his unwavering defense of those who were underprivileged. Despite his average academic performance and strong-willed opinions, or perhaps because of them, he attended and graduated from Emory and Henry College, a small Methodist College in Virginia. Although his liberal views were not well-received by the conservative college establishment, as an undergraduate, he participated in many anti-Vietnam War rallies and was a staunch anti-war advocate. After graduation, Kincheloe attended the University of Tennessee where he earned two Master's degrees, one in history and one in education. While there, he was transformed intellectually by his study of Paulo Freire's classic work, *Pedagogy of the Oppressed*, profoundly influencing the rest of his life. Kincheloe stayed at Tennessee for his doctoral program in educational history, which he completed in 1980. His research focused on evangelical camp meetings of fundamentalist Christians in the 1800s (Steinberg, 2009).

Kincheloe's early academic career expanded his thinking about disenfranchisement in American society. His first faculty job was in South Dakota at Sinte Gleska College, where he was appointed chair of the education department. While at Sinte Gleska, on the Rosebud Sioux Reservation, Kincheloe witnessed first-hand the disenfranchisement of Native Americans. He was given the name of *TiWa Ska*: "Clear Mind or Loving Mind or Brilliant Mind" a fitting appellation that reflected his life and work. Kincheloe next taught at Louisiana State University in Shreveport, where he helped start a doctoral program in curricular studies. His emerging research was so successful he was soon fast-tracked and recruited to Clemson University as a full professor. During a conference in 1989 in Dayton, Ohio, Kincheloe met Shirley Steinberg, a brilliant thinker and scholar in her own right. The two were an instant couple and became inseparable personally, professionally and intellectually until Kincheloe's death. Together they moved to university positions in Florida and New York before Kincheloe was asked to come to McGill University in Canada where, as chair, he, along with Shirley, founded the *Paulo and Nita Freire International Project for Critical Pedagogy* (Steinberg, 2009). The Freire Project is one of the world's most prominent think-tanks on promoting and promulgating the work of Freire and others in overcoming the oppression of poor people through education and empowerment.

RESEARCHER AND WRITER

Kincheloe's theoretical framework has been described as merging the democratic philosophy of John Dewey and the constructivist psychology of Lev Vygotsky (joekincheloe.com, 2008, p. 1). His work drew on a vast range of traditions, and was embedded in a rich eclectic research methodology that Kincheloe characterized as *bricolage*. This approach is rooted in a self-reflective and self-critical grasp of the relationship between a researcher's ways of seeing and the social location of his or her personal history.

As a promoter of critical constructivism, multicultural education, and contemporary curriculum discourses, Kincheloe was the architect of a cognitive theory that focuses on the development of a critical post-formal educational psychology. Post-formalism investigates and exposes the unexamined power relationships that shape cognitive theory and educational psychology. This liberatory effort to develop a psychology of possibility ultimately added a critical hermeneutic and historical epistemological dimension to the traditional process of learning. Moreover, Kincheloe stressed the relevance of contextualization in deriving meaning, which refers to the realization of the importance of the circumstances and settings within which meaning is created (Kincheloe, 2008b).

Kincheloe's ideology is captured in his book *Knowledge and Critical Pedagogy: An Introduction* (2008b), in which he critically questioned knowledge production, its purpose, access to it and its role in development. Citing the false premises used by President George W. Bush to initiate the American invasion and war with Iraq, Kincheloe revealed how "facts" were reported by various sources of information and manipulated into falsehoods he called "political knowledge" to justify an unjust war. Kincheloe suggested that educators should use the curriculum to explore the sources of knowledge, the rules of its production, and whether its intent is to cause harm to the truth or to oppressed people.

In this same text, Kincheloe referred to himself as a "vehement critique" who worked in the spirit of Paulo Freire's "radical love." He defined critical pedagogy as an approach to education that encourages students, first, to become conscious of the social oppressions or dominations around them (racism, sexism, etc.) and, second, to reflect on the actions that may be required to become free (emancipated) from those oppressions or dominations. In other words, Kincheloe concurred with the assertions of Henry Giroux that we are only free if we foster a climate whereby individuals are not afraid to question and challenge the dominant power structure (Kincheloe, 2008b).

Kincheloe questioned the traditional assumptions made in knowledge construction, which he found to be to be archaic, disempowering and morally objectionable. His called his major thesis, *Critical Constructivism*, noting that knowledge construction is contextual and arguing that the knowledge people possess is created using available cultural tools. Among his arguments he points out that the knower is a historical and social subject whose knowledge is shaped by his or her experience. For this reason, he advocated, education should facilitate understanding this context of knowledge construction rather than simply acquiring existing knowledge (Kincheloe, 2005, 2008b). And he challenged the dominant culture in America to be "concerned with white positionality in their attempt to understand the power relations that give rise to race, class and gender inequality...[and] to legitimate social/educational categories and hierarchal divisions" (Kincheloe & Steinberg, 1998, p. 3).

Joe L. Kincheloe spent his career expanding and expounding upon values he established as a child. With his passion and prolific writing ability, he is considered one of the greatest scholars of critical pedagogy of our time, particularly for his significant work in expanding the influence of Freire. In extraordinary ways, Kincheloe creatively enabled cognitive constructs and theoretical frameworks that allow us to better understand the darkness of oppressive forces and the critical importance of fostering liberty and justice for all.

REFERENCES

joe.kincheloe.com. (2008). *Joe. L. Kincheloe*. Retrieved from: http://joekincheloe.com/about

Kincheloe, J. (2008a). *Critical pedagogy*. New York, NY: Peter Lang Publishing.

Kincheloe J. (2008b). *Knowledge and critical pedagogy: An introduction*. New York, NY: Springer Science + Business Media.

Kincheloe, J. (2005). *Critical constructivism primer*. Peter Lang Publishing, Inc. New York, NY.

Kincheloe, J., & Steinberg, S. (1998). Addressing the crises of whiteness: Reconfiguring white identity in a pedagogy of whiteness. In J. L. Kincheloe, S. R. Steinberg, N. M. Rodriguez & R. E. Chennault (Eds.), *White reign: Deploying whiteness in America* (pp. 3–29). New York, NY: St. Martin's Griffin.

Steinberg, S. (2009). *Joe Kincheloe*. Retrieved from http://www.freireproject.org/content/joe-kincheloe-0

JERRY ALDRIDGE & JENNIFER KILGO

23. ALFIE KOHN

Critic of Traditional Schooling

Although Alfie Kohn is a major proponent of progressive and constructivist thought, he has also contributed to the field of critical pedagogy as a critic of traditional practices used in public education. Kohn holds a B.A. degree in interdisciplinary studies from Brown University and an M.A. degree in social sciences from the University of Chicago. A deep thinker and provocative writer, Kohn is the author of numerous books and articles, and lectures the world over on themes related to parenting, discipline and classroom management, as well as alternative approaches to schooling.

SUMMARY OF THOUGHT

The central core of Kohn's critical work can be explained by highlighting the following assumption regarding critical pedagogy. Certain types of knowledge are accepted and revered more than others. Further, school knowledge is "owned" by a privileged group who uses that form of knowledge to marginalize and exclude others; and, those in power use that power to maintain their dominant position in society, including the field of education (Christensen & Aldridge, 2013).

In the current climate of education, certain types of knowledge are valued over other types, as in the case of math and science being more revered than the social sciences and the arts. This kind of mindset unwisely fosters an order of emphasis as to which content area is more important than another. As a critic of an infrastructure that only places value on knowledge as defined by the dominant group, Kohn views the notion of curriculum more holistically and does not place it into separate entities, arguing that the curriculum should be more versatile based on student interest and teacher need. In other words, Kohn advocates for students and teachers constructing their own curriculum that centers around students' questions, problems, challenges, and projects as opposed to skill and drill, rote memory of facts and figures, and a narrow focus on selected subjects that are most valued by those in positions of power (Kohn, 1993).

Perhaps Kohn's greatest contribution to critical pedagogy involves his untiring criticism of standardized testing, which works as an institutional instrument in which the knowledge to be learned for the sole purposes of taking these standardized tests is that which is "owned" and controlled by the privileged group. This results in the

James D. Kirylo (Ed.), A Critical Pedagogy of Resistance: 34 Pedagogues We Need to Know, 89–92.

dismissal of other types of knowledge and the further control and marginalization of those who have been historically disenfranchised. In his books, *The Schools our Children Deserve: Moving Beyond Traditional Classrooms and "Tougher Standards* (1999) and *The Case Against Standardized Testing: Raising the Scores, Ruining the Schools* (2000), Kohn makes a compelling case about the inappropriate use of standardization and standardized tests. The critical themes of these books are highlighted in the paragraphs that follow.

Two of Kohn's primary criticisms of traditional schools that appear in his 1999 source are the back to the basics movement and the test-driven curricula that pervaded schools during the last decade of the 20th century and continue to dominate educational practices today. Instead, Kohn promotes a progressive approach to learning in which students construct their own knowledge and teachers serve as facilitators with the goal of guiding students to think critically. With Kohn's recommendations, grades would no longer exist and would be replaced by written narratives or performance reviews (Kohn, 1999).

In Kohn's 2000 text, he provides convincing evidence of the abuses and misuses of standardizes tests. The same individuals who create and mandate standardized tests, specific curriculum mandates, and tougher standards use their power to maintain their dominant position in society. Kohn provides impressive evidence that standardized tests are inextricably tied to economic status. Standardized tests measure upper middle class knowledge that is "owned" by those in power. Because of the uses and abuses of standardized tests alone, those in power conveniently and successfully use their power to oppress and exclude those who are not privileged to this cultural capital (Kohn, 2000).

In his book, *Punished by Rewards: The Trouble with Gold Stars, Incentive Plans, A's, Praise, and Other Bribes* (1993), Kohn artfully underscores the importance of equity and fairness within the classroom, explicitly railing against behavioristic approaches and the use of rewards and punishments when it comes to classroom management, discipline, and organization. Instead, he argues for alternatives that replace heteronomous practices with those that promote autonomy, fairness, and intrinsic motivation.

Kohn's rationale for encouraging autonomy for children in the classroom involves three benefits. The first benefit is a fostering of autonomy, which is "a more respectful way of dealing with others" (Kohn, 1993, p. 221). The second reason autonomy should be developed, according to Kohn, is that it encourages constructive and more meaningful interactions between students and teachers, which builds a more cooperative and collaborative climate in exploring the curriculum. Further, Kohn provides convincing evidence that promoting autonomy in the classroom actually works better than reward systems. Finally, Kohn (1993) believes that autonomous classrooms also promote fairness and intrinsic motivation as well.

Kohn does not stop there, but also describes unconditional parenting that promotes love and reason over rewards and punishment (Kohn, 2005). Kohn's approach in this source is quite different from other parenting guides that focus on striving for children to be obedient. The primary focus suggested is for parents to find out what their children need and then to seek ways to meet those needs. Kohn goes even further to describe how children require unconditional love with an understanding that we all occasionally make mistakes. He encourages parents to communicate to children that they are accepted even when they do not meet expectations. Finally, he recommends that parents must keep in mind the long-term goals for children that include becoming autonomous, responsible and caring adults (Kohn, 2005).

In his insightful text, *What to Look for in a Classroom...and Other Essays* (1998), Kohn thoughtfully explores the characteristics of a democratic classroom, explicitly describing concepts related to issues of power, equity, and justice. Once again, Kohn examines how rewards and punishments in classrooms create unequal power, causing students to be dependent on teacher judgment instead of developing their own sense of justice and autonomy. An example of this is highlighted in the chapter entitled, "A Lot of Fat Kids Who Don't Like to Read—The Effects of Pizza Hut's *Book It!* Program and Other Reading Incentives." Children who receive rewards, such as a pizza, for reading books results in a change in the power structure of the classroom and places the emphasis on teacher rewards instead of enhancing students' intrinsic motivation and autonomy. According to Kohn (1998), promoting equal power among teachers and students through collaboration is regarded as a most effective way to promote equity, justice, and caring dispositions in the classroom.

CONCLUSION

Regardless of the way in which Kohn interfaces with the field of critical pedagogy, his approach is decisively accessible, suggesting practical, well-researched approaches to education and parenting. He clearly bridges the gap between academia and popular culture, simultaneously appealing to a broad audience of scholars, practitioners, parents, and the public at large. Kohn's work not only appears in esteemed academic publications, but it can be found in newspapers, popular magazines, and the world-wide-web. The entire latter point is important because at times the writings of critical pedagogues often can be obscure and difficult to comprehend, monumentally limiting their audience with the risk that their work can be perceived as elitist. In the final analysis, Kohn's work significantly contributes to the thinking of critical pedagogy because it is grounded in equity, justice, and developmentally appropriate practice.

REFERENCES

Christensen, L. M., & Aldridge, J. (2013). *Critical pedagogy for early childhood and elementary educators.* Berlin, Germany: Springer Press.

Kohn, A. (1993). *Punished by rewards: The trouble with gold stars, incentive plans, A's, praise, and other bribes.* Boston: Houghton Mifflin.

Kohn, A. (1998). *What to look for in a classroom...and other essays.* San Francisco: Jossey-Bass.

Kohn, A. (1999). *The schools our children deserve: Moving beyond traditional classrooms and "tougher standards".* Boston: Houghton Mifflin.

Kohn, A. (2000). *The case against standardized testing: Raising the scores, ruining the schools.* Portsmouth, NH: Heinemann.

Kohn, A. (2005). *Unconditional parenting: Moving from rewards and punishments to love and reason.* New York: Atria Books.

PATRICIA A. CRAWFORD

24. JONATHAN KOZOL

Writer, Intellect, and Powerful Voice for the Marginalized

Jonathan Kozol is one of the most recognizable and widely known critical pedagogues of this generation. For nearly half a century, he has forcefully, tenaciously, and persuasively argued that the public school system in America is broken; that by its very nature it does not serve the needs of all children, particularly those who are Black, Hispanic, or poor. Rather, he argues, urban schools are too frequently constructed in ways that isolate, demean, and disenfranchise the very people they were intended to serve.

Like many critical pedagogues, Kozol's work has consistently addressed issues of race, class, equity, and hegemonic dominance. However, unlike many who work in the field, Kozol has chosen to position his work directly at the intersection of critical thought and popular culture. While many critical writings are aimed at an academic readership and characterized by a dense professional lexicon, Kozol has chosen to make his work accessible to a wide variety of readers. His style of writing is straight forward; his tone blending passionate and personal perspectives of life and schooling in some of the poorest areas in the United States. The result has been that the sharp, yet poignant, social critiques put forth in Kozol's work have reached an amazingly broad audience.

Kozol's work includes a National Book Award winner, Death at an Early Age: The Destruction of the Hearts and Minds of Negro Children in the Boston Public Schools (1967), as well as several New York Times best sellers, including Savage Inequalities: Children in America's Schools (1991), Amazing Grace: The Lives of Children and the Conscience of a Nation (1995), Ordinary Resurrections: Children in the Years of Hope (2000), and The Shame of the Nation: Restoration of Apartheid Schooling in America (2006). Few works related to critical pedagogy have received this type of recognition and acceptance among those in the academy and general public alike.

EARLY LIFE AND THE MAKING OF AN ACTIVIST

Jonathan Kozol was born on September 5, 1936. Reared in a Jewish Boston household, his father worked as a psychiatrist and neurologist and his mother as a social worker. From an early age, Kozol aspired to be a writer; a passion which led him to an Ivy League education. He enrolled in the English Literature program at

James D. Kirylo (Ed.), A Critical Pedagogy of Resistance: 34 Pedagogues We Need to Know, 93–96.
© *2013 Sense Publishers. All rights reserved.*

Harvard College, from which he graduated summa cum laude in 1958. A Rhodes Scholarship afforded him the opportunity to continue his studies at Oxford. Prior to returning to the United States, Kozol lived in Paris, where he honed his writing skills in both fiction and nonfiction, working alongside notable authors and social critics, such as Richard Wright (Raney, 1998; Shetterly, 2006).

Clearly, there is no single event that makes one an activist. However, when Kozol returned to 1960s America, he was confronted by the fervor of the Civil Rights Movement and by the passionate concern and activism demonstrated among young people. In particular, he was gripped by the 1964 murder of the three civil rights workers in Mississippi. As the injustice and horrific details surrounding this case emerged, Kozol felt compelled to respond in a tangible way. He did so by applying to teach reading at a freedom school in Roxbury, a key hub of Boston's Black community. It was here that he first gained direct experience with both the inequities that characterized segregation and the hope that comes from working directly with children. These factors drew him toward the goal of becoming a public school teacher and at least initially, away from the writing career to which he had aspired (Kozol, 1991; 2006; Raney, 1998).

In the fall of 1964, Kozol applied to be a teacher in the Boston public schools. With no teaching certificate, he was relegated to the role of substitute, eventually teaching the fourth grade. Kozol's journey during that year is well chronicled in *Death at an Early Age* (1967), in which he describes the shock of encountering a totally segregated system; one characterized by dangerous conditions, a lack of resources, prejudiced teachers, and a curriculum that held little relevance to the lives and learning of students. Kozol witnessed the crushing impact of this system on children's academic achievement, as well as on their mental health. He became convinced that the mis-education he witnessed was not a random act, but rather a systematic and political one, designed to maintain the status quo of a race and class segregated populace. Before the end of his first year, Kozol was fired for introducing the non-sanctioned poetry of Langston Hughes into the curriculum. *Death at an Early Age* received national acclaim shortly after its publication and continues to be a touchstone text today.

After leaving the Boston public schools, Kozol went on to teach in the wealthy public schools of Newton, Massachusetts. He then returned to Boston to work in the development of Free Schools, as an alternative to the public education system. He also used this opportunity to continue his writing and social justice work.

WRITING FOR CHANGE

In the years following the release of *Death at an Early Age,* Kozol's writing became characterized by the articulation of a more pronounced political stance. It was during this period that he began an enduring friendship with Paulo Freire. Like Freire's work, Kozol's writing emphasized the significance of emancipatory learning and encouraged educators to work collectively with students, families, and colleagues to effect change and promote social justice. Kozol investigated a number of educational models, both within and beyond the United States. His sharp critiques of American schools and positive reviews of some aspects of Cuba's literacy campaign were not received without controversy among conservative audiences (Kozol, 1975; 1978; 1982).

During the past 25 years, Kozol has framed school reform within the context of a larger need for social reconstruction. By probing such issues as homelessness in *Rachel and Her Children* (1989), adult illiteracy in *Illiterate America* (1985), and draconian public policies in *Amazing Grace* (1995), Kozol continues to demonstrate that inadequate schools are neither the sole cause, nor a mere result of poor educational systems. Rather, inequitable and ineffective schools are part of a much greater systemic problem; one in which education systems cannot be separated from their overall social context within society.

While many statistics are available about quality of life in impoverished areas, Kozol's writing offers a glimpse at the human faces and devastating experiences that accompany these numbers. He has been particularly effective in showing what it means to live at the intersection of racism and poverty by providing in-depth qualitative perspectives, which help readers to feel the lived experiences of the individuals featured in his books. His powerful narratives allow readers to understand the impact that diminished resources, security, and opportunities have on human lives. This is vividly portrayed in Kozol's (2012) most recent work, *Fire in the Ashes: Twenty-five Years Among the Poorest Children in America.*

Perhaps, most significant, is the fact that Kozol has offered readers persistent and uncomfortable reminders that America's social problems have not been solved, underscoring the stark reality that many schools and entire regions have become increasingly segregated and impoverished over time; demonstrating that ground has been lost, not gained, in the efforts to meet the needs of all citizens (Kozol, 1995; 2006). To that end, Kozol's work clearly challenges all critical pedagogues to never give up the struggle of championing social, economic, and educational justice for all children, and particularly for those who have been historically marginalized (Kozol, 2008). While Kozol's rhetoric has evolved over the years, the passion and urgency of his message have not.

REFERENCES

Kozol, J. (1967). *Death at an early age.* Boston: Houghton Mifflin.
Kozol, J. (1975). *Night is dark and I am far from home.* New York: Simon & Schuster.
Kozol, J. (1978). *Children of the revolution.* New York: Delacorte.
Kozol, J. (1982). *Alternative schools: A guide for educators and parents.* New York: Continuum.
Kozol, J. (1985). *Illiterate America.* New York: Doubleday.
Kozol, J. (1989). *Rachel and her children.* New York: Fawcett.
Kozol, J. (1991). *Savage inequalities: Children in America's schools.* New York: Crown.
Kozol, J. (1995). *Amazing grace: The lives of children and the conscience of a nation.* New York: Crown.
Kozol, J. (2000). *Ordinary resurrections: Children in the years of hope.* New York: HarperCollins.
Kozol, J. (2006). *The shame of the nation: The restoration of apartheid in America.* New York: Crown.

Kozol, J. (2008). *Letters to a young teacher.* New York: Broadway.
Kozol, J. (2012). *Fire in the ashes: Twenty-five years among the poorest children in America.* New York: Crown.
Raney, M. (1998). An interview with Jonathan Kozol. *TECHNOS Quarterly, 7*(3). Retrieved from http://www.ait.net/technos/tq_07/3kozol.php.
Shetterly, R. (2006). *Americans who tell the truth.* New York: Dutton.

JAN LACINA

25. DONALDO MACEDO

The Socio-political Nature of Language

Donaldo Macedo is professor of English and a Distinguished Professor of Liberal Arts and Education at the University of Massachusetts Boston. Internationally recognized for his critical analysis on the interplay of power and language, Macedo has published extensively in the areas of linguistics, critical literacy, and bilingual and multicultural education. In this chapter, three prevailing themes within Macedo's published work are discussed: language, power, and ethnic/racial identity.

LANGUAGE

Drawing on the work of Labov, Preston, Tucker and Lambert, Shuy and Williams, Fraser, Freire, and others, Macedo particularly examines the socio-political aspects of language and how linguistic features often serve as social identifiers that may trigger stereotypes. In short, language stereotypes are a central focus of Macedo's work, challenging readers to rethink language and linguistic structures, especially for those groups of people who continue to be marginalized by society. In one of his early studies, he conducted an experiment to verify the findings of Tucker and Lambert in which speech samples from various Portuguese ethnic groups were used. The experiment involved studying the language attitude phenomenon among the Portuguese ethnic groups studied, focusing on overt and covert discrimination practices among the various dialect speakers. Macedo theorized that there are stereotypical attitudes toward certain dialect speakers—primarily which correlate with the socioeconomic status of the speaker's dialect spoken. With his experiment, judges from four Portuguese ethnic groups listened to tape recordings of eight speakers of Portuguese reading a passage. The speakers included dialects of the following: Continental, Brazilian, Capeverdean, and Azorean. Of the speakers, half were college educated and half had a fourth grade education. The data from the experiment revealed that judges recognized the ethnic, educational, and social class differences among the speakers' spoken language. Those speakers who had a limited amount of education were rated lower than their more educated peers (Macedo, 1981). This study, and much of his other work in this area, validates the unfortunate stereotypical practices relating to language. Indeed, Macedo's thought on language significantly contributes to the literature by critically analyzing language from a sociolinguistic perspective.

James D. Kirylo (Ed.), A Critical Pedagogy of Resistance: 34 Pedagogues We Need to Know, 97–100.
© 2013 Sense Publishers. All rights reserved.

In his book *Dancing with Bigotry* (1999), Macedo highlights the politics of language and its role in multicultural education, arguing that within the field of multicultural education, there is a dominant, paternalistic viewpoint of teaching tolerance. In teaching tolerance, educators are reinforcing the notion of trying to get along, instead of teaching ways for developing mutual respect across cultures. Macedo makes clear that racism and xenophobia are prevalent in today's world with the rise in immigration in many countries around the globe. For example, he describes in France examples of xenophobia as a result of immigration, particularly those immigrants who are Muslim from French colonies—and the challenges faced in France for this group of people. In Germany, the Turks faced a similar backlash with house bombings and not being recognized as full-fledged citizens. In summary, Macedo articulates that teaching tolerance does not address the necessary critical tools needed to understand how language is used in society and the way in which language structures devalue cultural and language groups. Throughout his work, he posits the need for critical literacy—to help educators re-think language structures and stereotypes, and the power that language holds in society.

POWER

Throughout his work, Macedo draws on his experiences as a Cape Verdean immigrant from West Africa and the challenges he faced in a monolingual higher education system. He explains what he calls *common culture literacy* as a form of the dominant culture, which is a limiting type of literacy because it primarily focuses on Western heritage values, and negates the experiences of the disenfranchised. In his book, *Literacies of Power: What Americans are not Allowed to Know* (2006), where the term *stupidification* is used throughout, Macedo demonstrates the ways in which schools, the media, and other institutions perpetuate a sense of ignorance. Moreover, particular with respect to the Reagan and Bush eras, he views those in political power as the teller of lies. And not leaving citizens off the hook, Macedo also faults U.S. voters for not demanding that Reagan tell the truth regarding his economic plan—and places the same blame on supporters of Bush.

Reagan's campaign centered on promises to balance the budget, cut taxes, and increase military spending. Since the Reagan era, U.S. voters can still see a continuation of balancing the budget used as a slogan for votes especially in the campaign slogans of presidential candidates; yet, since Reagan's time—we have reached a much greater economic desperation—with liberals and conservatives both failing. As Macedo calls this the power of stupidification—voters elect an official into a position of power with the promise of economic turn-around, and the promise of a balanced budget; yet, U.S. voters do not hold the elected official accountable to the campaign promise made. Macedo also connects stupidification to the U.S. school system, and one such example is when a young adolescent faced disciplinary action from his school because he failed to recite the Pledge of Allegiance. The young boy, David Spritzler, found the pledge as hypocritical. Spritzler's disciplinary action was spared when the American Civil Liberties Union wrote a letter on his behalf. Macedo clarifies that he find it incomprehensible that David's teachers and administrators cannot see through the hypocrisy of the Pledge of Allegiance, and he views such recitation as indoctrination. Educators can connect indoctrination throughout the media as well—when teachers with a political passion push only one viewpoint. This one sided type of instruction does our children a disservice—and does not enable them to learn how to think critically, to see the world from multiple viewpoints.

While Macedo's thought is naturally left-leaning, audiences not only from the left side of the aisle, but also from those on the right, can garner great insight on his analysis of power structures. According to Macedo, people in power, from whatever side of the aisle, often have a certain amount of control of their constituents—and in many cases manipulate and tell lies to get what they want—primarily for campaign votes. Consequently, Macedo's thoughts on power provide a critical examination of education and the politics involved, particularly on behalf of those who are poor and marginalized. In the end, he challenges educators, and, indeed, the public at large, to pay close attention to the politics of education, to resist indoctrination, and to create a schooling environment that fosters critical thought.

ETHNIC/RACIAL IDENTITIES

Macedo is also internationally known for his work analyzing mass media and news reports and the complex dynamics between ethnic and racial relations within the U.S. His work is unique in that he explains racism, and divisions among races, as not belonging to only hate based groups, but he also makes the case for such divisions within mainstream America. Macedo supports that one must move beyond monolithic constructs of Whiteness and Otherness to better understand the complexity of ethnic and racial relationships within the U.S. For example, he provides various examples within the media, especially of such extremist behaviors from radio talk show host Rush Limbaugh and former Louisiana gubernatorial candidate David Duke, that illustrate the dehumanization of various ethnic and cultural groups. Clearly, there is a media promotion of such radicalism—and unfortunately—there are those who have the inability to perceive falsifications of reality and for whatever reason do not have the knowledge or possess the tools to critically analyze reality.

Macedo worked very closely with Paulo Freire for many years. He co-authored articles and books with Freire, as well as translated much of Freire's work. Just as Freire's work is grounded in humility, great insight, and intelligence (Kirylo, 2011), Macedo's work is profound in its own right. Donaldo Macedo is a leader in the field of critical literacy. He challenges all of us to critically analyze media messages, to pay attention to the interplay of language and power, and to celebrate our cultural, language, and ethnic differences. In other words, "It is necessary to dare to speak of difference as a value and to say that it is possible to find unity in diversity" (Bartolome & Macedo, 1997, p. 222)

REFERENCES

Bartolome, L. I., & Macedo, D. P. (1997). Dancing with bigotry: The poisoning of racial and ethnic identities. *Harvard Educational Review, 67*(2), 222–246.

Kirylo, J. D. (2011). *Paulo Freire: The man from Recife.* New York: Peter Lang.

Macedo, D. P. (1981). Stereotyped attitudes toward various Portuguese accents. *National Clearing House for Bilingual Education, 4,* 2–9.

Macedo, D. P. (2006). *Literacies of power: What Americans are not allowed to know.* Denver, CO: Westview Press.

Macedo, D. P., & Bartolome, L. I. (1999). *Dancing with bigotry: Beyond the politics of tolerance.* NY: St. Martin's Press.

MATTHEW DAVID SMITH & ARTURO RODRIGUEZ

26. PETER MCLAREN

A Marxist Humanist Professor and Critical Scholar

BRIEF BACKGROUND

Peter McLaren was born and raised in Toronto, Ontario, Canada later spending time in Winnipeg, Manitoba. He attended public schools eventually earning a Bachelor of Arts degree in Elizabethan Drama from the University of Waterloo, later receiving a Bachelor of Education at Teachers College from the University of Toronto. He completed a Master of Arts degree at Brock University and ultimately a Ph.D. from the Ontario Institute of Studies in Education, University of Toronto. While conducting his early graduate work, in 1974, McLaren began a five-year career in the Jane-Fitch Corridor of Toronto. These experiences became the basis for his first book, *Cries from the Corridor* (see McLaren, 2006) which became a bestseller and sparked much debate across Canada on the issue of school reform. That book would later become an integral piece of the critically acclaimed *Life in Schools: An Introduction to Critical Pedagogy in the Foundations of Education* (2006).

At the conclusion of his doctoral work, McLaren published the critical ethnographic work *Schooling as a Ritual Performance: Towards a Political Economy of Educational Symbols and Gestures* (1999). Currently in its third edition that text continues to stand as one of the leading critical ethnographies in education. Following the publication of that work, McLaren served one year as special lecturer at Brock University, later moving on to a teaching post at Miami University in Oxford, Ohio where he began a lifelong friendship with Henry A. Giroux. It was when McLaren joined the faculty of the Graduate School of Education and Information Studies at the University of California, Los Angeles (UCLA) that his reputation as a prolific writer, provocative professor, a tireless speaker, and an unflinching supporter of overcoming value production took on a worldwide scope. His epistemic and philosophical transition from his appreciation of postmodernism to that of a Marxist Humanist marks a dramatic shift in the project that is his life's work.

THREE PIVOTAL WORKS

While McLaren has written prolifically and voluminously, and to be concise, we limit our examination to the critical themes of what can be considered his pivotal

James D. Kirylo (Ed.), A Critical Pedagogy of Resistance: 34 Pedagogues We Need to Know, 101–104.
© *2013 Sense Publishers. All rights reserved.*

works and what collectively captures the central core of his thought, *Life in Schools: An Introduction to Critical Pedagogy in the Foundations of Education* (2006), *Che Guevara, Paulo Freire, and the Pedagogy of Revolution (2000)*, *Schooling as a Ritual Performance: Towards a Political Economy of Educational Symbols and Gestures (1999)*.

LIFE IN SCHOOLS: AN INTRODUCTION TO CRITICAL PEDAGOGY IN THE FOUNDATIONS OF EDUCATION

Currently in its fifth edition, *Life in Schools* stands as one of the definitive works on education where McLaren interrogates capitalism and its hold on US public education. Throughout this text, McLaren invites students, teachers, community activists, and others to consider a critical society free from labor exploitation, racism, jingoism, and a myriad of other forces of oppression; a society in the commodification of labor is in a post-capitalist, communitarian society, one that accepts the human condition of all. Amidst the Bush Presidency's war on seemingly everything, McLaren's theoretical outlook, to burn through the fog of neoliberal capitalism so common amongst "progressive" educators, beckons all who dare engage his work to critically reflect on their own praxis. In *Life in Schools*, McLaren offers an analysis and theoretical reflection of the events portrayed in his first book *Cries from the Corridor*. He further traces the origins of critical pedagogy in the United States and abroad and explores some of the central tenets of the critical tradition. Ultimately, McLaren poses tough questions about public education: what roles do schools play in society? Are they purveyors of knowledge or do they indoctrinate students with the norms of an exploitative, capitalist class? Can schools be sites of social transformation, a radical consideration of praxis that enacts a world in which hegemony is undone? Finally McLaren calls for a global society in which we first consider human dignity, the natural environment, racial and gender equality in overcoming value production, the commodification of the human spirit.

CHE GUEVARA, PAULO FREIRE, AND THE PEDAGOGY OF REVOLUTION

In the most translated of McLaren's work, readers are presented with a comparative analysis of the life and work of two distinct pedagogues for revolution. One hailing from Rosario, Argentina, Che Guevara enjoyed a comfortable upbringing and medical education, later shedding the comforts of class for solidarity with the oppressed. An unrelenting combatant against the exploitation of the poor, el Che called for a world in which the existence of capitalism ceased. The other, Paulo Freire, from Recife, Brazil, a man who came of age while faced with the challenges of hunger and labor exploitation. Freire left law, short of practicing, to dedicate his time to education working with peasants who were illiterate in northeast Brazil. Freire began to develop the notion of "reading the world and the word" as he developed a literacy campaign with the overexploited communities in Brazil. For Freire literacy praxis placed at center the lived experiences of the students and teachers as the basis for their curriculum. Such revolutionary work, McLaren writes, prompted the Brazilian military and government to mark Freire as a subversive. After enduring a 70-day imprisonment for his teaching and writing, Freire entered a 16-year exile which McLaren describes as "tumultuous and productive" (2000, p. 145). McLaren's depiction of Guevara and Freire humanizes the two icons without essentializing or diluting their work. In the closing pages, McLaren presents an exploration on teaching, pedagogy, critical pedagogy, and revolutionary pedagogy. The popularity of *Che Guevara, Paulo Freire, and the Pedagogy of Revolution* may be found in the understanding that overcoming capital will not happen within the confines of capital; that is, Che and Freire knew full well the (maniacally intelligent and ever-changing) rules of capitalism will only lead to its reproduction. Alternatives to capitalism must come from persons and their shared vision of a new society.

SCHOOLING AS A RITUAL PERFORMANCE: TOWARDS A POLITICAL ECONOMY OF EDUCATIONAL SYMBOLS AND GESTURES

Originally McLaren's dissertation, *Schooling as a Ritual Performance* broke new ground in the areas of critical ethnography and sociology of education and anthropology. Now in its third edition, *Schooling as a Ritual Performance* has become a foundational text for investigating the links between schooling, socialization, and the larger economy. McLaren investigates the inner dynamics of rituals, or how the physical and psychological rites of passage of a working-class Catholic school in Toronto, Canada serve as tools for indoctrinating youth ensuring capitalist exploitation. Much of the analytical framework running through *Schooling as a Ritual Performance* is drawn from the work of Victor Turner. Moreover, this text offers readers a window to the theoretical and practical style of McLaren; he does not shy away from the messiness of social science research, but, rather, embraces a critical subjectivity weaving a symphony that harmonizes research with criticality. Through a significant focus on the theoretical analysis of everyday school processes, McLaren considers daily practice as the influencing component that leads the process of socialization. McLaren's criticality is evident in his evisceration of the smallest details. Part of the timelessness of *Schooling as a Ritual Performance* is McLaren's notion of the teacher as "liminal servant;" the liminal servant is one who unhesitatingly operates in the ambiguous spaces with a student population enduring a myriad of oppressive realities.

ROOTED IN MARXIST THOUGHT

Much of McLaren's current work originates in Marxist humanism. McLaren adheres to a tradition that includes Raya Dunayevskaya, Georg Lukacs, Karel Kosik, the Frankfurt School, and Paulo Freire (among many others). Marxist humanism draws much of its theoretical foundation primarily from the earlier writings of Marx.

Such works involve Marx and Engels laying out the foundations for an analysis of historical materialism, alienation, and false consciousness. Marxist humanism is oppositional to the structuralism proposed by Louis Althusser. Furthermore Marxist humanists draw from the work of Hegel for his notion of dialecticals. In dialectics we seek to overcome the exploitative relations of power, or the unity of opposites. In capitalism, the most fundamental unity of opposites is that of labor and capital: capital cannot exist without labor; thus it is in the best interest of capitalists to maintain the exploitative relationship whereby labor's role in the production of capital is one of servitude. In that light, labor therefore seeks to abolish capital. (This is not to be understood as the abolition of the *capitalist*, for the capitalist operates in the ways he or she has been conditioned. Freire (1970) reminds us that we always have the option to operate in solidarity with the oppressed). McLaren thus engages Marxist humanism as a means of analysis considering the interrelations of transnational neoliberal capitalism, public education, and the exploitation of the worldwide masses. The march toward overcoming a legacy of capitalist oppression necessarily involves the use of advanced theoretical tools, particularly those tools that operate outside of the bounds and confines of the oppressive system itself.

REFERENCES

Freire, P. (1970). *Pedagogy of the oppressed.* New York: Continuum.
McLaren, P. (1999). *Schooling as a ritual performance: Towards a political economy of educational symbols and gestures.* (3rd ed.). New York: Rowman & Littlefield.
McLaren, P. (2000). *Che Guevara, Paulo Freire, and the pedagogy of revolution.* New York: Rowman & Littlefield.
McLaren, P. (2006). *Life in schools: An introduction to critical pedagogy in the foundations of education.* (5th ed.). Boston: Allyn & Bacon.

WILLIAM CRAIN & KATHLEEN E. FITE

27. MARIA MONTESSORI

Advocate for Tapping into the Natural Curiosities of Children

Montessori schools have become a fixture in the U.S. and many parts of the world. Many parents want their children to benefit from the materials and methods Maria Montessori developed. Indeed, Montessori schools for young children are so common that a person unfamiliar with educational history would be surprised to learn that Montessori once challenged the educational mainstream. What's more, her underlying philosophy is still quite radical today.

EARLY LIFE AND WORK

Maria Montessori was born in 1870 in the province of Ancona, Italy. Her father was a civil servant and her mother was a homemaker. But while her mother's own life was conventional, her mother didn't want to see gender barriers hold Montessori back--a message that Montessori enthusiastically received. When Montessori was seriously ill as a 10-year-old, she told her anxious mother, "Do not worry, Mother, I cannot die; I have too much to do" (Kramer, 1976, p. 28). At the age of 26, Montessori became the first woman in Italy to earn an M.D. degree (Kramer, 1976).

During her early medical work, Montessori took an interest in children with developmental delays and challenged the prevailing view that they could not be educated. When she saw children in a barren room eagerly grab for bread, it occurred to her that they weren't actually hungry for food, but for cognitive stimulation. Adopting methods developed by Jean-Marc Gaspard Itard and Édouard Seguin, she began giving the children tasks such as beads to thread and cloth to button, and she found the children worked hard on them. Guessing they liked objects that could be physically touched and handled, she introduced literacy by giving them wooden letters that they could run their hands across. By such methods, she taught many of the children to read and write as skillfully as typical school children of the same age (Kramer, 1976).

In 1907, Montessori founded a school for 3- to 6-year-old children who lived in a tenement in an extremely poor section of Rome. In this school, called *La Casa dei Bambini*, Montessori experimented with sensorial and physical tasks like those she first used with the developmentally delayed children, and she also tried out new tasks. Once again, Montessori accepted the challenge of educating children who were generally deemed uneducable, and once again she achieved notable success.

James D. Kirylo (Ed.), A Critical Pedagogy of Resistance: 34 Pedagogues We Need to Know, 105–108.

Montessori's accomplishment soon inspired the creation of similar schools in many parts of the world. In the U.S., however, the initial enthusiasm was short lived. Her work was perceived as a threat to that of John Dewey and was roundly criticized. In 1914, the influential William Heard Kilpatrick, a Dewey disciple, issued a sweeping dismissal of her ideas, and public interest in Montessori receded until the late 1950s. Interest resurfaced largely because Americans sought educational tools to compete with the Russians. But few appreciated her fundamental ideas, a situation that still exists today.

AN INNER URGE TO LEARN

In conventional education, policy makers assume it's their job to set goals and expectations for children. Montessori, however, attempted to suspend her own ideas about what children should learn and, instead, to pay attention to children's own tendencies. She concluded that children have a deep inner urge to develop certain capacities and will work with amazing concentration on tasks that enable them to do so. She told, for example, about a 4-year-old girl who focused intently on putting different-sized cylinders into the holes of a wooden frame. The child repeated the task 42 times, completely oblivious to her surroundings. To test the child's concentration, Montessori had other children march and sing loudly, but the girl persisted with the task. When she finished, she smiled happily, as if emerging from a pleasant dream (Montessori, 1966).

Montessori observed such behavior again and again. After deep concentration, children emerged serene and happy. It seemed to Montessori that they were at peace because they had been able to develop an emerging capacity within themselves. Montessori found that deep concentration often occurs when children are free to choose their tasks. Children seek out the kinds of tasks they need, as if led by an inner guide. In contemporary Montessori schools, the core materials are largely set, but the schools place considerable emphasis on children's free choices (Montessori, 1949/1967b; Crain, 2011).

AGAINST CONFORMITY

In conventional schools, it is assumed that adults must motivate children to learn. When children "perform" well, adults give them praise, gold stars, and high grades. When children "perform" poorly, adults criticize them and tell them to work harder. Montessori opposed all such extrinsic inducements. She wanted children to learn from their own inner impulse to develop their powers and from their curiosity about the world. The deepest thought, she believed, comes when one is passionate about one's work and loses oneself in it. Grades, criticism, and other inducements actually hinder such thinking; children frequently become so anxious about how well they are doing that they cannot concentrate deeply. Moreover, external rewards and punishments undermine children's independence. Children become so preoccupied with the "right" answers—the answers that meet with adult approval—that they no longer think for themselves. They become conformists who will never dare to criticize the established social order. Thus, Montessori removed all external motivators—even praise—from the classroom. Learning comes from inner desire (Montessori, 1948/1967a).

ALIENATION FROM NATURE

In the last half of the 20th century, Rachel Carson (1954/1998), Theodore Roszak (1972), and others called attention to the modern individual's alienation from the natural world. More recently, Richard Louv (2005) and others (Crain, 1997) have described how this situation is particularly worrisome for children, who need rich contact with nature to grow well. Montessori saw the problem early on. In *The Montessori Method* and *The Discovery of the Child*, published in 1909 and 1948, respectively, Montessori described children's intrinsic interest in nature and how we adults isolate them from it. She said we have become contented prisoners in the artificial world of our own making and have passed this prison down to our children. She urged us to let children walk with bare feet on the wet grass; run outside in the rain; and, take all the time they need to observe animals, which fill them with wonder. She also urged educators to provide children with opportunities for gardening and animal husbandry. Rich experiences with nature, she said, stimulate children's powers of patient observation and promote a loving attitude toward life. Deprived of contact with nature, children become lethargic and unhappy.

CHILDHOOD ASSESSMENT

Contemporary education is dominated by the standards movement, which constantly presses for higher scores on standardized tests. It often seems that test scores are all that matter. Montessori, in contrast, placed little value on exams and test scores. To her, what are important are children's emotions and attitudes toward learning. She valued children's curiosity, independence, concentration, happiness, serenity, and love of life—qualities that are largely untapped by standardized tests (Crain, 2011).

CONCLUDING COMMENT

Montessori's work had its limitations. Above all, Montessori didn't appreciate children's play, fantasy, and artistic activities. She knew children spontaneously took to these activities, but she was more interested in children developing their intellectual skills (Crain, 2011). Perhaps Montessori secretly felt that the children she was teaching most urgently needed intellectual skills to compete with their wealthier peers. In any case, contemporary Montessori schools increasingly make room for play, fantasy, and the arts because the children themselves have a deep inner desire to engage in these activities. By doing so, contemporary educators adhere to Montessori's most fundamental principle: Follow the child's own deepest urges.

REFERENCES

Carson, R. (1998). The real world around us. In L. Lear (Ed.), *Lost woods: The discovered writings of Rachel Carson*. Boston, MA: Beacon Press. (Work originally published 1954.)

Crain, W. (1997, Spring). How nature helps children develop. *Montessori Life, 9*, 41–43.

Crain, W. (2011). *Theories of development: Concepts and applications* (6th ed.). Upper Saddle River, NJ: Pearson.

Kramer, R. (1976). *Maria Montessori*. Reading, MA: Addison-Wesley.

Louv, R. (2005). *Last child in the woods*. Chapel Hill, NC: Algonquin.

Montessori, M. (1964). *The Montessori method* (A.E. George, Trans.). New York: Schocken. (Work originally published 1909).

Montessori, M. (1966). *The secret of childhood* (M. J. Costelloe, Trans.). New York: Ballantine. (Work originally published 1936).

Montessori, M. (1967a). *The discovery of the child* (M. J. Costelloe, Trans.). New York: Ballantine. (Work originally published 1948.)

Montessori, M. (1967b). *The absorbent mind* (C. A. Claremont, Trans). New York: Holt, Rinehart & Winston. (Work originally published 1949.)

Roszak, T. (1972). *Where the wasteland ends*. Garden City, NY: Anchor.

CHANDNI DESAI & RUBÉN GAZTAMBIDE-FERNÁNDEZ

28. EDWARD SAÏD

An Exilic Pedagogue

Palestinian scholar Edward Wadie Saïd was an *exilic* pedagogue. Throughout his expansive body of work, Saïd called for intellectuals to exist in metaphorical exile by engaging in dissent, to daringly resist authority and hegemonic thinking, to speak against injustice, and to work with integrity to provide alternative perspectives against dominant thought (Saïd, 1994). While Saïd was not a scholar of education in the traditional sense, he was without a doubt a committed educator, and his work has been profoundly influential on critical education scholarship, particularly with respect to post-colonial thinking.

Saïd's own experiences of exile and movement across multiple national and cultural borders and his sense of being "never quite right, and indeed very wrong and out of place" marked his extensions of exile as a metaphor for intellectual work (2000a, p. 87). Born in Jerusalem on November 1, 1935, Saïd lived a dissonant life, stuck between many disparate worlds. Though secular, he was born into a Christian-Palestinian family and was raised in both Palestine and Egypt. He was educated at Princeton and Harvard, and later tenured at Columbia University, where he spent most of his academic career. However, it was not until the 1967 Arab-Israeli Six-Day War that Saïd fully realized his exilic tenets and commitments, leading to a perpetual sense of dislocation and a life-long commitment to the Palestinian struggle (Saïd, 2000a).

It was out of these experiences of exile that Saïd's post-colonial thinking and critical pedagogy came to life in the tenets that constitute the "exilic intellectual." Saïd's pedagogy demands that one ask questions, fight on the side of the oppressed, and reject orthodoxies of opinion in the quest toward interrogating power, thereby bringing light to that which hides beneath the surface. "Speaking the truth to power," argued Saïd, "is carefully weighing the alternatives, picking the right one, and then intelligently representing it where it can do the most good and cause the right change" (1993, p. 102). In his work, this commitment was evident in three particular ways: analysing the role of imperialism in the production of knowledge about the "Orient"/ Other; articulating a contrapuntal textual analysis for unravelling power relations; and, developing a praxis towards decolonization, freedom, and justice.

James D. Kirylo (Ed.), A Critical Pedagogy of Resistance: 34 Pedagogues We Need to Know, 109–112.

ORIENTALISM: EMPIRE AND THE PRODUCTION OF KNOWLEDGE

Saïd's exilic pedagogy is first expressed in his ground-breaking and widely influential 1978 book *Orientalism*. In this text, Saïd demonstrates how the colonial politics of domination gain power and legitimacy through the production of knowledge about "the Other," in this case, about "the Orient." Through his analysis of the emergence of "Orientalism" as both the academic study as well as the literary representation of "the Orient," Saïd demonstrates the role of knowledge production as a technology of power through which imperialist violence is justified. Saïd argues that the Orient was constructed ahistorically through European imaginations of geography and of the people who inhabited it. According to hetero-masculinist European imaginings, the Orient became a place where all non-white bodies became essentialized as either exotic or as dangerous and always-already "backwards."

Key to Saïd's argument is not only how the production of knowledge about the Orient/Other is imperative for consolidating imperial rule, but for the production of an evolving European subjectivity. For Saïd, the West/Occident produces itself— its identity and culture—through the invention of the East/Orient as its antithesis. "The construction of identity," argued Saïd, "involves the construction of opposites and 'others' whose actuality is always subject to continuous interpretation and re-interpretation of their differences from 'us'" (1978, p. 332). Saïd's analysis in *Orientalism* gained prominence and was embraced by scholars across a wide range of disciplines during the early eighties, particularly in the emerging field of post-colonial studies. Methodologically, *Orientalism* opened the door for a radical analysis of colonization and imperialism in the study of race, gender, class, sexuality, and culture, and it continues to be relevant around the world.

READING CONTRAPUNTALLY: UNRAVELLING POWER, CULTURE, AND IMPERIALISM

In *Culture and Imperialism* (1993), Saïd contends that colonization is not simply about the acquisition of territory. Rather, it is impelled by cultural formations that included the belief that certain people and places required domination. The process of geographic domination involves the production of ideas about those who inhabit the spaces to be colonized. Saïd makes a compelling point about the nature and complexity of the challenge, emphasizing that "none of us is completely free from the struggle over geography ... because it is not only about soldiers and canons but also about ideas, about forms, about images and imaginings" (1993, p. 7). Saïd demonstrates how the European cultural imaginary plays a central role in the construction of White supremacy and the justification of imperialism through the conquest of distant territories, justified under the guise of improving and civilizing the "others." Such analyses become central to the role of the exilic intellectual, whose task is "first distilling then articulating the predicaments that disfigure modernity— mass deportation, imprisonment, population transfer, collective dispossession, and forced migration" (1993, pp. 332–333). Such a task requires a different approach to the analysis of various texts, what Saïd called a "contrapuntal" reading.

As a response to hegemonic power and ideas, contrapuntal readings produce a critical counter discourse to empire, by exhuming that which is beneath the surface as a way to oppose the colonizing force of every text. Borrowing the term from European classical music, for which Saïd had a deep affection, a contrapuntal reading offers a counter voice that does not simply "accompany," but rather inflects the "melodic" movement of the dominant voice with dissonance and delays resolution in an "atonal ensemble" (1993, p. 318). A contrapuntal reading provides a different contextualization and understanding of cultural texts that addresses the perspectives of imperialism and resistance. Central to this reading practice is situating the text within the social and political world in which the work is produced in order to historicize and interrogate it for its sociality and materiality. As a practice, a contrapuntal reading "goes directly against the grain of readings and writing to erect barriers between texts or to create monuments out of texts," as is the case in disciplinary canonical projects (2000b, p. 137). Pedagogically, contrapuntal reading enables the unravelling of that which is under the surface by paying attention to the hierarchies and power-knowledge nexus embedded in them through an interrogation of history and the assumptions that uphold traditional curriculum and pedagogy.

THE PRAXIS OF DISSENT: DECOLONIZATION, FREEDOM AND JUSTICE

Saïd's work has had a profound influence on the evolution of ideas within post-colonial studies. Rather than suggesting the end of colonization, Saïd's post-colonial scholarship positioned the exilic subjects that emerge out of colonization at the centre of a praxis toward decolonization. For Saïd, decolonization means resisting the colonizer by using various tactics for liberation, including an understanding of violence as a response to colonial rule. It also requires a certain kind of analysis directed inward toward the colonized self. Since the concept of nationalism was central to anti-colonial struggles, inward criticism for the colonized nation was extremely important to Saïd. Though he was one of the most prominent voices for Palestinian rights, freedom and self-determination, his thinking around nationalism shifted over time. That is, while Saïd was an advocate of Palestinian nationalism, he was critical of the internal contradictions of nationalism when it became a tool for ruling national elites that mimicked imperialism. In response, Saïd's praxis shifted toward co-existence. He envisioned Palestinian decolonization and "lasting peace" to the Israeli-Palestinian conflict through co-existence between Israelis and Palestinians in a secular, bi-national, democratic state that was based on equals rights and citizenship for all people. This shift in position led to death threats, and both false accusations of anti-Semitism as well as the banning of his books in the Occupied Territories of the West Bank and Gaza. However, he remained committed to exposing the plight of Palestinians to the Western world, influencing the ongoing

Palestinian struggle for self-determination, and the international solidarity movement in their calls for justice, freedom and equality.

While the struggle against oppression and injustice inspired most of Saïd's intellectual work, he was also equally inspired by music and is considered an important music critic. In the early 1990s Saïd met the renowned Argentinian-Israeli pianist and conductor Daniel Barenboim. While they stood on opposite ends of the struggle, Saïd and Baremboim had similar visions about peaceful co-existence in Israel-Palestine. Together they created the West-Eastern Divan Orchestra, a workshop that brings together young musicians from Israel and various countries in the Middle East. The project was established to hone musical talent and create a forum for cross cultural dialogue, reflection, and co-operation. Though they both recognized that music in and of itself would not resolve the Israeli-Palestinian conflict, they envisioned the orchestra as an alternative model that encouraged people across difference and in conflict to bridge ideas, work together, express themselves, and listen to one another (Barenboim & Saïd, 2002).

At the age of sixty-seven, on September 25, 2003, Edward Saïd died from leukemia in New York. While he has physically departed from the world, his legacy lives on. His vision for decolonization, equal and peaceful coexistence continues to live through the Orchestra as it serves as a symbol for a different Middle East. His theories, methods, and exilic pedagogies continue to be used among many critical educators committed to justice and social change.

REFERENCES

Barenboim, D., & Saïd, E. (2002). *Parallels and paradoxes: Explorations in music and society.* New York: Pantheon Books.
Saïd, E. (2000a). *Out of place: A memoir.* New York: Vintage Books.
Saïd, E. (2000b). *Reflections on exile.* Massachusetts: Harvard University Press.
Saïd, E. (1994). *Representations of the intellectual.* New York: Vintage Books.
Saïd, E. (1993). *Culture and imperialism.* New York: Vintage Books.
Saïd, E. (1978). *Orientalism.* New York: Vintage Books.

COLE REILLY

29. IRA SHOR

Shoring up Pedagogy, Politics, and Possibility
for Educational Empowerment

BRIEF BACKGROUND

Born in 1945 to a working-class, Jewish family, Ira Shor was raised in a rent-controlled apartment in the South Bronx, surrounded by many other Eastern European families. Both his parents were first-generation Americans, each the descendants of Russian immigrants. At 15, Ira's father dropped out of school and went on to build US battleships and aircraft carriers as a sheet-metal worker throughout WWII and the Korean War. Ira's mother graduated but, despite all efforts to continue on to college, she could not afford it; instead she worked as a bookkeeper.

Throughout the 1950s and 1960s, Ira's lived experiences as a working-class, second-generation American in the South Bronx influenced his evolving thinking and politics regarding discrimination as well as other matters related to social justice – themes that would remain prevalent throughout his career. Likewise, these formative years shaped and informed his ideas regarding education and the role of teacher(s) and/or school(s). For his elementary and junior high years, Ira attended what might be described as a mediocre public school; however, his being granted entry into the esteemed New York City's Bronx High School of Science proved to be an eye-opening experience for him. Never before had he been made so keenly aware of the blatant inequalities between the rich resources and opportunities afforded to the *haves* at more prestigious institutions, when compared with the subpar, *have-not* conditions at poorer schools. If schools were to reflect a microcosm of their respective communities, his k-12 experience was certainly a tale of two cities: one wrought with a poverty of prospects and woebegone circumstances, and the other draped in affluence, opportunity, and access-abundance.

FREIREAN INFLUENCE

The 1960s proved to be an especially exciting time for Shor to grow and explore as both a student and scholar of life. After high school, he went on to earn a BA in English from the University of Michigan in 1966, later followed by an MA and PhD through the University of Wisconsin. Particularly during the turbulent years of the mid-1960s and into the early 1970s, Shor participated in a number of U.S.

James D. Kirylo (Ed.), A Critical Pedagogy of Resistance: 34 Pedagogues We Need to Know, 113–116.

antiwar, civil rights, and students' rights movements. With his studies informing his politics and vice versa, 20th century American writer and critical leftist intellectual, Kurt Vonnegut, provided Shor considerable inspiration, fueling the focus of his dissertation. And while Vonnegut certainly played a major role in Shor's thinking, it was when he was introduced to the work of the Brazilian educator, philosopher, and scholar, Paulo Freire, that his thinking became more crystallized.

Freire's groundbreaking *Pedagogy of the Oppressed* (1970) remains undisputed as foundational to the literary cannon of the critical pedagogy movement. [Freire's later works (e.g., 1973, 1978, 1985, 1995, 1997; Shor & Freire, 1987) are significant as well.] As Shor embarked on his journey as a university professor during the 1970s, clearly influenced by Freire's work, he passionately began employing his own interpretation of Freirean theory with his working-class students at Staten Island Community College as well as at City University of New York (CUNY). Particularly through his composition and rhetoric courses, Shor explored with his students the dialectical interweaving of theory and practice and how Freirean principles of critical pedagogy and literacy might operate in praxis. Through modeling and promoting a healthy, epistemological relationship with all subject matter – something Shor insists teachers develop – he folded social critique of the status quo into his instruction and strove to awaken such latent thinking in his undergrads. Working in concert with his students, Shor developed a number of pedagogical innovations to empower a co-creation of new educational possibilities in each course. Collectively these efforts worked to produce a more thoughtful, just, and democratic educational experience, effectively subverting certain hegemonies of authoritarianism and teacher-centeredness, replacing those with problem-posing pedagogies that were dialogical and constructivist in nature.

CRITICAL PUBLICATIONS

Nearly a decade of such [above] efforts evolved into Shor's *Critical Teaching and Everyday Life* (1980), the first book-length adaptation published of Freirean critical pedagogy and what many consider Shor's breakthrough contribution to the field of critical pedagogy. With this book, Shor provided a thoughtful synthesis of his early discoveries at CUNY when first experimenting with liberatory teaching. To no surprise, Shor regards this stage of his life/career with particular fondness as it afforded a mutual transformation for his working class students and himself; through a dialogical climate they explored themes from the classroom and everyday life. To all this Shor provides a politically conscious, critical analysis of schooling in general (formally and otherwise) as a construct of democratic opportunity for empowerment as well as growth.

Having read Shor's book, Freire was clearly moved, so much so that he initiated a correspondence with Shor in 1982 (first by letter, then phone), and soon the pair had arranged to meet, leading them to become longtime friends and collaborative partners. Most notably, they joined forces on *A Pedagogy for Liberation: Dialogues on Transforming Education* (1987), which is an extraordinary book that naturally focuses on critical themes related to an education that is liberating. This text has been republished numerous times and in various languages. Within a dozen years of its publication, Shor went on to write two other books focusing explicitly upon making Freire's work and thinking more accessible to others around the globe (1987, 1999a). Few could deny that for years to come (1986a, 1986b, 1992, 1996) and even after Freire's death in 1997 (1999b, 2006, 2007; Shor & Pari, 1999a, 1999b, 2000), vestiges of their landmark partnership remain in Shor's writing.

What distinguishes Shor's contribution as a curricular scholar and critical pedagogue is his fervent and infectious idealism for education as a vehicle toward authentic empowerment. As such, he embraces a uniquely constructivist and dialogical pedagogy, challenging students and teachers alike to consider how they might indeed be responsible to *change* their world, rather than merely adapting themselves to accommodate existing social structures or submitting to reproducing existing hegemonies of injustice. All this calls for an epistemological approach to knowledge and how it is (de)constructed as well as a significant shift in terms of embracing a hybridic discourse – neither one entirely academic nor of the everyday. Shor's classroom is predicated upon a new and organic idiom of communication, where the traditional trappings of power for teachers and subordinate scripts for students are abandoned in lieu of a more learning-centered, curious, and unapologetically controversial experience of meaning-making as exploration.

CONCLUSION

The fact that Ira Shor has remained at CUNY for more than forty years is indicative of a commitment to his community roots, which is clearly driven by a critical pedagogical process and one that is framed in social justice work *as* praxis. As Shor (2006) puts it, "my classes are diverse in color, ethnicity, age, and majors, requiring me to learn each class's profile and offering one of the few multi-racial 'contact zones' to test critical learning in our society" (p. 30). Might his contemporaries choose any number of cushier positions or posts, relaxing into retirement with the sense of ease and accomplishment afforded them? Certainly, and many do, but Shor sees [and seizes] his classroom and his pen with all the opportunity and empowerment they might afford. An exception to the apparent rule among many celebrated curricular scholars and critical pedagogues, Shor indeed practices theory as much as he theorizes practice.

Says Shor (2006), "For me, it's learning for civic activism, knowledge making that orients people to question their society..." (p. 35). Problem-posing dialogue and putting social constructivism into action – these principles remain at the center of his own teaching and learning. Ever mindful of the realities and complexities associated with striving to teach in such a manner, Shor's work is nothing if not forthcoming of how delicate a task and artful a craft critical pedagogy is to truly employ. In truth, he struggles (and will continue to struggle) throughout that process himself. Still he rejoices in the rich harvest it yields for his students, for him, and for us all.

REFERENCES

Freire, P. (1970). *Pedagogy of the oppressed*. New York, NY: Seabury.

Freire, P. (1973). *Education for critical consciousness*. New York: NY Seabury.

Freire, P. (1978). *Pedagogy in process*. New York, NY: Continuum.

Freire, P. (1985). *The politics of education: Culture, power, and liberation*. Westport, CN: Greenwood Press.

Freire, P. (1995). *Pedagogy of hope: Reliving pedagogy of the oppressed*. New York, NY: Continuum.

Freire, P. (1997). *Pedagogy of the heart*. New York, NY: Continuum.

Shor, I. (1980). *Critical teaching and everyday life*. Chicago, IL: TheUniversity of Chicago Press.

Shor, I. (1986a). *Culture wars: School and society in conservative restoration*. Chicago, IL: The University of Chicago Press.

Shor, I. (1986b). Equality is excellence: Transforming teacher education and the learning process. *Harvard Educational Review. 56* (November), pp. 406–26.

Shor, I. (Ed.). (1987). *Freire for the classroom: A sourcebook for liberatory teaching*. Portsmouth, NH: Heinemann Press.

Shor, I. (1992). *Empowering education: Critical teaching for social change*. Chicago, IL: The University of Chicago Press.

Shor, I. (1996). *When students have power: Negotiating authority in a critical pedagogy*. Chicago, IL: The University of Chicago Press.

Shor, I. (1999a). *Education is politics: Paulo Freire's critical pedagogy*. In P. McLaren and P. Leonard (Eds.). *Paulo Freire: A critical encounter*. New York, NY: Routledge.

Shor, I. (1999b). What is critical literacy? In I. Shor & C. Pari (Eds.), *Critical literacy in action: Writing words, changing worlds*. Portsmouth, NH: Heinemann Press.

Shor, I. (2006, Winter). Wars, lies, and pedagogy: Teaching in fearful times. *Radical Teacher. 77*, 30–35.

Shor, I. (2007, Summer). Teaching notes: Can critical teaching foster activism in this time of repression? *Radical Teacher. 79*, 39.

Shor, I., & Freire, P. (1987). *A pedagogy for liberation: Dialogues on transforming education*. Westport, CN: Greenwood Press.

Shor, I., & Pari, C. (Eds.). (1999a). Critical literacy in action: Writing words, changing worlds. Portsmouth, NH: Heinemann Press.

Shor, I., & Pari, C. (Eds.). (1999b). *Education is politics: Critical teaching across differences, K-12*. Portsmouth, NH: Heinemann Press.

Shor, I., & Pari, C. (Eds.). (2000). *Education is politics: Critical teaching across differences, Postsecondary* Portsmouth, NH: Heinemann Press.

ANN ELISABETH LARSON

30. SHIRLEY STEINBERG

Unwavering Commitment to Social Justice

Teacher, intellectual, scholar, innovator, provocateur, improviser, and champion for social justice, Shirley Steinberg has demonstrated a long-standing, unwavering commitment to examining how power is situated within social and cultural contexts. Indeed, through her scholarly work and socio-political action, Steinberg is a powerful advocate for just change, possibility, and improvement of the human condition. Currently, a professor of Youth studies at the University of Calgary and Director and Chair of The Werklund Foundation Centre for Youth Leadership, Steinberg's pro-active engagement in the global community is nothing short of remarkable. She is the author and editor of numerous books and articles which focus on themes related to cultural studies, critical pedagogy, urban and youth culture, and popular culture. And, many of these publications have been with her beloved late partner and collaborator, Joe Kincheloe, both of whom are co-founders of *The Paulo and Nita Freire International Project for Critical Pedagogy*.[1] Steinberg is a frequent media contributor and has been honored with numerous national and international awards.

CRITICAL THOUGHT

As one who studied Steinberg's work in graduate school and as a participant in her sessions at a variety of international conferences, what is strikingly clear of Steinberg's disposition is her ability to inspire those of us in education and other disciplines to embrace the role of what it means to be an agent of change. A significant aspect to Steinberg's thought is to take seriously the notion of what it means to be "critical" and its link to pedagogy, praxis, and educational thought, all of which is sometimes not deeply explored in teacher education programs. In other words, Steinberg's work provokes contemplation and a commitment to action that transcends traditional boundaries of theory-to-practice orientations in education and certainly in teacher education.

For example, as a response to conventional societal achievement norms such as the bell curve which have unfairly and inaccurately differentiated cultural groups, Steinberg's extension of multiculturalism to what she characterizes as critical multiculturalism is a call for teachers to adopt pedagogies that push the intersection of power, identity and knowledge and move learning and experience

James D. Kirylo (Ed.), A Critical Pedagogy of Resistance: 34 Pedagogues We Need to Know, 117–120.

to emancipatory change (Kincheloe, Steinberg, & Gresson, 1997). Her edited text, *Kinderculture: The Corporate Construction of Childhood* (2011a) coined the term kinderculture, which has become part of the popular cultural lexicon and is based on a critical theory critique of the extremity of capitalistic influences on children in contemporary society. Kinderculture also critically describes the commodification of early childhood, violated by a corporate culture that emphasizes consumerism over nurturing children's genuine interest, choice and independent thought in their interaction with a world where privilege is often confused for ability.

Media Literacy: A Reader (2007), co-edited with Donald Macedo, has proven to be a popular text in teacher education language and literacy methods courses and in applied English courses (National Council Teachers of English, 2012). The text promotes a position that while many believe that humans exercise and adopt agency, they are, in truth, recipients and agents of a myriad of social, cultural, and political influential forces. The media is a powerful contributor to these forces and affects how humans make sense of the world and act through behavior and decision-making. Media literacy creates a participatory culture in which people who live in a global society experience opportunities for civic engagement, artistic and cultural expression, fluid dialectical exchange, and informal mentoring. Through these interactions, Steinberg emphasizes the power of social connections, which are formed in multiple media modalities through affiliations, expression, collaborative problem solving, and circulation of knowledge and ideas, thus resulting in a more highly empowered conception of what it means to be a citizen in the modern world (Steinberg, 2010). Moreover, Steinberg challenges educators to consciously attend to the dynamics and complexity of education in a democratic society, which is under continuous threat in a policy environment that pushes simplistic political views and approaches for reform (Steinberg & Kincheloe, 2006).

In their compelling work, *A Tentative Description of Post-Formal Thinking* (Kincheloe & Steinberg, 1993) and *The Post-formal Reader* (Steinberg, Kincheloe, & Hinchey, 1999), the authors argue a theory of post-formalism, contending that although 20th century psychology, including Piagetian and post-Piagetian theory, is acknowledged for significant advancement in the field of psychology, "a time for reassessment" has arrived. That is, while neo-Vygotskian theories and analyses and situated cognition have risen as primary tenants within the discipline of cognitive psychology, the texts claim that the interactions and connections between social and psychological dimensions of learning theory and educational psychology are essential in educational studies. The authors point to post-formal thinking as a theory that concerns questions of meaning and purpose, multiple perspectives, human dignity, freedom, and social responsibility. Building upon the work of numerous scholars in the field of curriculum theory and curriculum studies, post-formalism calls upon teachers to guide learners to critically inquire, to uncover hidden assumptions, to observe relationships, to deconstruct what they observe and experience, to connect logic and emotion, and to attend to context. To be sure, an infusion of post formalism theory into educational course activities, experiences, and assessments holds promise to bring communities of learners together around what is, and what could be right with the world.

Other of Steinberg's works and collaborations, *Teaching Teachers* (2004); *Teen Life in Europe* (2005); and, *Cutting Class: Socioeconomic Status and Education* (2007) have collectively illuminated the powerful point that those who work in education in whatever capacity should embrace with full awareness and grounding of what critical pedagogues are compelled to do in their work, which is fundamentally to examine, unpack and reconstruct the curriculum they teach, creating a critical culture for learning where students are active agents in their striving toward the making of a more hopeful, democratic world. It is in that context, that classrooms become empowering spaces for both educator and student.

CURRENT FOCUS

Continuing on with a common theme that has threaded the trajectory of her life's work, Steinberg's most current scholarly efforts have been intensely focused on the cultural, social, and education development of youth. Using leadership as a framework to enhance the capabilities and life successes of young people, Steinberg's work, through *The Werklund Foundation Centre for Youth Leadership Education*, shows promise for impactful, translational scholarship and practice that may well turn the tide of numbers of disaffected and disassociated young people in our troubled, complicated 21st Century world. Her work and advocacy for youth and her concerns about how society views young people is a clarion call particularly for educators to positively and constructively support young people to participate more fully as democratic agents within society.

Finally, with Steinberg's examination related to research methodology, it is clear that she has significantly contributed to the thinking of qualitative research (Steinberg, 2011b; Steinberg & Cannella, 2012). Her scholarship encompasses provocative intersections of educational theory and thought, making stronger the opportunities for researchers to employ complex single and mixed-methodology studies, which enhances communities of practice within the field of educational research, all of which naturally coalesces around civic, cultural, scientific, anthropological, ethnographic, and other areas of the human condition. Indeed, Steinberg's desire to promote more diverse forms of qualitative research, and to deeply emphasize sociocultural context is a natural response to the positivist ideology that has for so long dominated mainstream policy-making.

Steinberg's scholarship is ultimately based on an exploration of culture, social issues, and education, provoking consideration on how educators teach, communicate, and critically reflect upon their work so that the learner and educator move toward a deeper understanding of self in the collective movement toward a more liberated world. Uniquely provocative and influential for education studies and a wide-range of other disciplines, Steinberg's scholarship illuminates ambiguities and contradictions. She interweaves historical, philosophical, cultural, and social thought to contextualize education, with the goal of posing an emancipatory and transformative perspective for educators to transform their work in schools. Indeed, Steinberg's unwavering commitment to social justice continues to challenge and inspire educators the world over.

NOTES

[1]   The Paulo and Nita International Project is a virtual and literal archive of global initiatives in critical pedagogy, deeply committed to the study of oppression in education and how issues of race, class, gender, sexuality, and colonialism shape the nature and purpose of education. Rooted in the thinking and spirit of Paulo and Nita Freire, the project supports an evolving critical pedagogy that encounters new discourses, new peoples, new ideas, and continues to move forward in the 21st Century. Indeed, the project has established itself as a global community of researchers and cultural workers who collectively possess as their aim to promote a more just and democratic world for all (http://www.freireproject.org/).

REFERENCES

Kincheloe, J. L., & Steinberg, S. R. (1993). A tentative description of post-formal thinking: The critical confrontation with cognitive theory. *Harvard Educational Review*, *63*(3), 296–320.

Kincheloe, J. L., & Steinberg, S. R. (Eds.). (2007). *Cutting class: Socioeconomic status and education.* New York, NY: Rowman and Littlefield Publishers.

Kincheloe, J. L., Steinberg, S. R., & Bursztyn, A., (Eds.). (2004). *Teaching teachers: Building a quality school of urban education.* New York, NY: Peter Lang Publishing.

Kincheloe, J. L., Steinberg, S. R., & Gresson, A. D. (Eds.). (1997). *Measured lies: The bell curve examined.* Palgrave Macmillan: UK.

National Council of Teachers of English (2012). Retrieved from: http://www.ncte.org/search?q=macedo+

Steinberg, S. R. (Ed.). (2005). *Teen life in Europe.* Westport, CT: Greenwood Press.

Steinberg, S.R. (Ed.). (2010). *19 urban questions: Teaching in the city* (2nd Ed.). Peter Lang: New York.

Steinberg, S. R. (Ed.). (2011a). *Kinderculture: The corporate construction of childhood* (3rd ed.). Boulder, CO: Westview Press.

Steinberg, S. R. (2011b). Critical pedagogy and qualitative research: Moving to the bricolage. In Denzin, N., & Lincoln, Y. (Eds.). *The Sage handbook of qualitative research* (4th ed.). (pp. 163–178). Thousand Oaks, CA: Sage Publications, Inc.

Steinberg, S. R., & Cannella, G. S. (Eds.). (2012). *Critical qualitative research reader.* New York, NY: Peter Lang Publishing.

Steinberg, S. R., & Kincheloe, J. L. (Eds) (2006). *What you don't know about schools.* Macmillan: UK.

Steinberg, S. R., Kincheloe, J. L., & Hinchey, P. (Eds.). (1999). *The post-formal reader: Cognition and education.* New York, NY: Routledge.

Steinberg, S. R., & Macedo, D. (Eds.). (2007). *Media literacy: A reader.* New York, NY: Peter Lang Publishing.

BASANTI D. CHAKRABORTY

31. AUNG SAN SUU KYI

Pedagogue of Pacifism and Human Rights

Ultimately our aim should be to create a world free from the displaced, the homeless and the hopeless, a world of which each and every corner is a true sanctuary where the inhabitants will have the freedom and the capacity to live in peace.

Suu Kyi, 2012

INTRODUCTION

Aung San Suu Kyi, a practitioner of peaceful mediation, received the 1991 Nobel Peace Prize while under house arrest in Burma, now present Myanmar. The story of her life is intertwined with the lives of the Burmese people and their struggles for freedom and human rights. A brief glimpse into the life of Aung San Suu Kyi reveals the path of a peaceful leader in the making. She was born on June 19, 1945 in British Burma. Her father, General Aung San, was an advocate of democracy and freedom. Assassinated when Suu Kyi was only two years old, General Aung San was a national hero in Burma. Suu Kyi's mother was an active member of a political group known as Women's Freedom League.

Suu Kyi grew up surrounded by various leaders and generals, taking in all the stories of the many heroic deeds of her father. Her mother, Ma Khin Kyi, joined the Burmese Parliament after her husband's death and later became the country's first minister of Social Welfare, later appointed as ambassador to India. Naturally moving with her mother to India, it was there that Suu Kyi studied the writings and teachings of Mahatma Gandhi. In 1964 Suu Kyi went on to study at Oxford University, and later went on to work at the United Nations.

It was in 1988 while Suu Kyi was visiting Burma to nurse her mother who suffered a stroke that she became painfully aware of the socio-political situation the people of Burma were enduring. Ne Win's Burma Socialist Program Party (BSPP) was in power at that time. The majority Burmese people did not have enough food to eat and were devoid of other facilities like plumbing, electricity, and the use of telephones. When Burmese students rebelled against Ne Win, he not only ordered the closing of universities and enacted night curfews, but also silenced their call for freedom by placing them in prison. The Burmese people lived in fear, repression, and were tortured. And while peaceful protesters were arrested and troops fired

James D. Kirylo (Ed.), A Critical Pedagogy of Resistance: 34 Pedagogues We Need to Know, 121–124.
© *2013 Sense Publishers. All rights reserved.*

at the unarmed activists, leading to many deaths, Ne Win could not suppress the movement. Protestors became more energized and widespread; building so much pressure that Ne Win was forced to call for an election to decide Burma's future. However, Ne Win's overture to hold an election was predictably wrought with fraud as the process was not fair and free. In short, BSPP was not willing to give up power, leading the people of Burma to suffer through years of military repression under the military rule. On August 8th, 1988, known as the massacre 8–8-88, 3,000 Burmese people were slaughtered while holding a peaceful demonstration.

TURNING POINT

Suu Kyi could not remain silent. She sent a letter to the Ne Win's BSPP party suggesting to form a government to usher an era of free multi-party elections. She urged non-violence, and suggested the government to release all prisoners who were held during the demonstration. While Suu Kyi's proposals were accepted by political activists, BSPP remained silent, prompting Suu Kyi to join a protest where she addressed a massive crowd in front of Shwedagon Pagoda, a sacred Buddhist temple of Burma. Addressing the rally Suu Kyi proclaimed, "I could not as my father's daughter remain indifferent to all that was going on. This national crisis could in fact be called the second struggle for national independence" (Suu Kyi, 1991, page 193). Continuing on, she urged the people to remain focused on their goal of success through discipline and unity, clearly arousing the mass gathering.

The electrifying speech clearly had an inspirational effect on the people, thrusting Suu Kyi as the unofficial leader of their resistance movement. As a consequence, the people's opposition grew stronger resisting military repression that eventually the BSBP party was abolished and a new council-the State Law Order Restoration Council (SLORC) was created. While this council ordered curfew, banned public gatherings, and suggested a temporary period of military control, it promised free fair elections will be held after the establishment of law and order in the country. Suu Kyi had her doubts about SLORC's promises and began collaborating with other freedom movement leaders in order to create a political party. With Suu Kyi as the general secretary, the National League for Democracy (NLD) was created. As Suu Kyi toured the country setting up units of the NLD party, tens of thousands of people were inspired to join. As general secretary, she spoke against military killings, imprisonments, and violations of human rights. She not only appealed to the United Nations and international human right organizations, but she also urged ambassadors of other countries and heads of states to condemn military violence against the peaceful unarmed people of Burma.

In May, 1989, the government announced a date for general election and Suu Kyi's name appeared on the ballot of NLD party. Even though universities were reopened after the killing of students in 1988, the restrictions on public gatherings and meetings were still enforced. Yet, under Suu Kyi's determined leadership, the people and the political parties raised their voices against the suppression of human rights and decided to hold protest marches to honor leaders including Suu Kyi's father, the deceased General Aung San through a Martyr's Day event. However, fearing the killing of innocent people, Suu Kyi took the decision to cancel the event. Despite her house arrest and intimidation by military junta, Suu Kyi continued her struggle for the cause of the people and human rights.

In July 1991, Suu Kyi was awarded Sakharov prize for *Freedom of Thought*, and in October of that same year, she was awarded the Nobel Peace Prize. However, she did not leave Burma to receive the award fearing that the SLORC government will not allow her to return to Burma. The publication of Suu Kyi's book *Freedom from Fear* (1991), during her house arrest, served as a powerful voice against oppression to the rest of the world. The writings poignantly depicted the course of the country's struggles from the days of Suu Kyi's illustrious father, to the mass killings of innocent people, including university students of the 1988 massacre; and finally her house arrest that resulted in an international outcry of protest against the suppression of human rights. Suu Kyi was released from house arrest in 2010 and in April 2012 she was elected to Parliament in a landslide victory.

CONCLUSION

Suu Kyi was painfully aware of the actions of powerful leaders that subjected innocent people of Burma through torture, genocide and inhuman treatments. Yet, throughout the course of the freedom struggle, never was she tempted by the provocations and intimidation of the military junta. Instead, she remained resilient only to prove that non-violence is not cowardice; rather, it is the courage of grace and peace. In the changing context of the life and the pursuit of liberty of all oppressed peoples, Suu Kyi's critical pedagogical approach transcends geographic boundaries and touches the core value of humanity where violence has no place. As is in the case of Mahatma Gandhi, Nelson Mandela, Martin Luther King, Jr., and others, Suu Kyi serves as a sterling example for peace educators around the world. She can be characterized as a non-traditional critical pedagogue who, through her unwavering commitment to the cause of human rights, paved the path of liberation for the Burmese people. Indeed, Suu Kyi demonstrated genuine leadership through her courage, determination, and personal sacrifice, reaffirming the belief that peaceful means of resistance is a powerful force against oppression, injustice, and inequality.

REFERENCES

Aung San Suu Kyi (2012). Retrieved on September 09, 2012, from The Official Website of the Nobel Prize: http://www.nobelprize.org/nobel_prizes/peace/laureates/1991/kyi-lecture_en.html
Aung San Suu Kyi (1985). *Let's visit Burma*. London: Burke Publishing Company.
Aung San Suu Kyi (1991). *Freedom from fear.* New York: Penguin Books.
Ling, Bettina (1999). *Aung San Suu Ki: Standing up for democracy in Burma*. New York: The Feminist Press at The City University of New York.
Amnesty International (http://www.amnesty.org)
Free Burma Organization (http://www.FreeBurma.org)
Human Rights Watch (http://www.hrw.org)

RENÉE M. CASBERGUE

32. LEV SEMENOVICH VYGOTSKY

The Mozart of Psychology

INTRODUCTION

Lev Vygotsky was relatively unknown among western psychologists and educators until well after his death, and is now arguably one of the most influential theorists to shape modern views of learning and development. His research career ended only ten years after he made the first presentation of his work in 1924; he died of tuberculosis in 1934 at age 37. While his scholarly work was highly regarded in pre- and post-revolutionary Russia, it was not until almost 40 years after his death that his theories were widely circulated outside of that country. Beginning in the 1960s, his work has profoundly influenced education in the United States and around the world.

For many, the name Lev Vygotsky immediately brings to mind his concept of the Zone of Proximal Development. Yet his contributions to the field of psychology were numerous, varied and always groundbreaking. From his perspectives regarding thought and language to his assertion that learning leads development, Vygotsky never hesitated to swim against the tide of current scientific thought. What is known of his brief life offers insight into how Vygotsky developed the keen, creative mind that led eminent psychologists many years his senior to describe him as an "outstanding scholar," a "genius," and notably, "the Mozart of Psychology" (Toulmin, cited in Vygodskya, 1995).

Born in 1896 in the small town of Orshe in what is now Belarus, Vygotsky's family was recognized as one of the most highly educated in the city; his mother was trained as a teacher and his father was one of the founders and most active members of the local Society of Education. After receiving primary level education at home with a private tutor, Vygotsky enrolled in an all boys private secondary school in Gomel where he excelled at mathematics, literature, and philosophy, and later went on to medical school at Moscow University, although he soon decided to pursue a law degree instead. It was while enrolled in that program that his love of literature was rekindled. While completing his law degree, he enrolled simultaneously in the historical-philosophical division of Shanavsky University, a progressive institution that, while awarding degrees, was not officially recognized by the government. Vygotsky pursued a degree there purely to satisfy his desire to be immersed in literature and the humanities. It was at that institution that he also developed an interest in psychology at the age of 19. That would become a lifelong passion.

James D. Kirylo (Ed.), A Critical Pedagogy of Resistance: 34 Pedagogues We Need to Know, 125–128.

After graduating from both universities in the same year, he returned to Gomel where he soon became a teacher of literature and humanities, prompting him to ponder why some children seemed to learn more easily than others, some to develop more quickly, and some to require more assistance. He found that the popular contemporary theories of development and learning at the turn of the century offered inadequate support for his observations, leading him on a journey to forge new psychological theory (Vygotsky, 1978). Vygotsky's presentation of three research reports at a 1924 prestigious conference in Russia won him significant acclaim, which immediately prompted a research position offer at the Moscow Institute of Experimental Psychology. At the age of 27, his life work became a pursuit of critical questions that dramatically reshaped theories of learning and development (Vygotskya, 1995).

RECONCEPTUALIZING LANGUAGE AND THOUGHT

Vygotsky's theories challenged widely accepted notions of learning in important ways. Among his earliest departures from current orthodoxy were his theories regarding language and thought. While theorists of his time viewed language and thought as separate processes, with language at most a tool used to communicate already constructed thoughts, Vygotsky viewed language and thought as symbiotic processes. He was most interested in the *relationship* between thought and language and the ways that each shaped the other. From a Vygotskian perspective, thought cannot exist without language; thoughts can never be fully formed or understood until the words are found to express them. And in the process of using language to develop thoughts, language itself grows through the web of interconnected meanings reflected in expanding thought (Vygotsky, 1986).

RECONCEPTUALIZING LEARNING AND DEVELOPMENT

In a similar vein, Vygotsky also questioned established authority regarding the relationship between learning and development. Prominent psychologists of his time, most notably Jean Piaget (born the same year as Vygotsky), posited that development always preceded learning. That is, children had to achieve certain levels of developmental capability for learning to occur. That perspective is reflected in the widespread belief well past the middle of the 20th century that children younger than six could not be taught to read, for example, because they would not yet have developed sufficient levels of symbolic thought. To the contrary, Vygotsky theorized that learning precedes and leads development through the use of language as a cultural tool. From his perspective, learning occurs through interactions with others and with objects in the environment. These interactions result in two forms of learning: everyday concepts gained through a child's own observations and experiences, and "scientific" concepts – the kind of knowledge in which children must be "schooled" (Kozulin, 1990).

Vygotsky believed that a reliance on observation of children's everyday or spontaneous concepts alone led to the faulty notion of development as a precursor to learning. When children's progress in learning scientific concepts was considered, psychology then had to account for learning that could only occur through interaction with the environment mediated by someone more knowledgeable about the scientific content. Vygotsky's observation of that type of learning, beginning with reflection on his own learning aided by his childhood tutor, and continuing through his early teaching career, led him to assert that children were capable of learning concepts that took them beyond previously achieved development, and that, in fact, such learning nudged development forward. Thus, helping children consider abstract or symbolic thought enables them to engage in abstraction and symbolism in ways that were previously beyond their capability. In this way, learning leads development.

THE ZONE OF PROXIMAL DEVELOPMENT

Vygotsky's ideas about thought, language, learning, and development culminated in his most widely cited theory – that of the Zone of Proximal Development (ZPD). As interactions among learners and more capable others assumed a central role in Vygotsky's views of cognition, he pondered *how* those interactions prompted learning and development. From his work as a teacher and researcher, Vygotsky recognized that children were capable of learning concepts beyond their developmental capability if they were provided guidance in the form of questions or prompts from someone more knowledgeable. Vygotsky theorized that if a learner received such support, he or she would internalize new knowledge and be able to apply it to perform more independently when the same or similar problem-solving situations later arose.

Hence, a "teacher" – who could be anyone with more knowledge such as a peer, a parent, a tutor – would be most effective if he or she recognized the learner's current level of understanding and offered just the right amount of support to move that understanding forward. He described the ZPD as "the distance between the actual developmental level as determined by independent problem solving and the level of potential development as determined through problem solving under adult guidance in collaboration with more capable peers" (Vygotsky, 1978, p. 86).

VYGOTSKY'S IMPACT ON EDUCATION

Vygotsky's theories have profoundly influenced the field of education. Perhaps because he was himself a teacher, Vygotsky's understanding of how children learn and the best ways to teach them continues to resonate with educators today. His thinking undergirds many current beliefs about learning and development. The very notion of individualizing instruction to meet the needs of learners, entrenched in modern concepts of differentiated instruction, dynamic assessment, and response to intervention approaches, derives from Vygotsky's insight that not all children can be assumed to need the same type of instruction simply because their ages suggest a particular stage of development. Teaching methods that encourage hands-on, experiential learning, with the teacher serving as a resource to further children's thinking and concept development, reflect Vygotsky's perspective that learning is social and occurs through interactions with the environment and those with more knowledge. And the current emphasis on vocabulary learning, language development, and comprehension – especially in early childhood – suggests acceptance of Vygotsky's theory about the interconnectedness of thought and language.

Although Vygotsky lived a very short life filled with the tragic losses of two brothers and his mother at an early age, his stature as an eminent scholar is far greater than his span of years. While it has been nearly 80 years since anyone was able to hear his voice, he still speaks with authority in the 21st century.

REFERENCES

Kozulin, A. (1990). *Vygotsky's psychology: A biography of ideas.* Cambridge, MA: Harvard University Press.

Vygodskya, G. L. (1995). His life. *School Psychology International, 16*(2), 105–116.

Vygotsky, L. (1978). *Mind in society: The development of higher psychological processes.* Cambridge, MA: Harvard University Press.

Vygotsky, L. (1986). *Thought and language.* Cambridge, MA: MIT Press.

PETER ROBERTS

33. SIMONE WEIL

Education, Spirituality and Political Commitment

The French thinker Simone Weil has seldom been considered part of the critical pedagogy story, yet there is much in her legacy of potential interest to scholars and practitioners in this area. Weil died at the tragically young age of 34, leaving behind a body of mostly unpublished writings that would later influence others in fields as diverse as classical studies, literature, philosophy, sociology, politics, and theology. She had a comprehensive grasp of different traditions of thought in the humanities, but she was also at home in mathematics and the sciences. Shaped by the cultures of the West, she nonetheless had great respect for the insight offered by Eastern sages. Weil combined her formidable intellect with a staunch commitment to those whom she regarded as less fortunate than herself. She was, in addition, an innovative and 'subversive' school teacher, rubbing against the grain of educational orthodoxy in attempting to best serve her students.

BACKGROUND

Born in 1909, Weil was raised in a middle class Parisian family. Despite her relative privilege, she was aware of the hardships faced by others and felt a strong sense of solidarity with them (McLellan, 1990). At just five years old, she declared that she would go without sugar as an act of solidarity with those similarly deprived on the front line. Later, she would refuse to wear socks, noting that many workers had to go without them (Fielder, 2001). Her adolescence was characterized by hard work, headaches, and despair. She felt herself to be inferior to her brother André, a gifted mathematician, but her own scholarly abilities were such that upon leaving school and attending the *École Normale Supérieure*, she emerged at the top of her class.

After completing her studies, Weil became a teacher. In her work with students in Le Puy, she quickly found herself in trouble with school authorities. Weil was opposed to the prevailing pedagogy of rote learning. She wanted students to value education beyond the instrumentalist goal of preparing for examinations. She also saw that the world of learning was not confined to the classroom and sometimes took her students outside to expand their educational horizons. She fostered a spirit of creativity, questioning and inquiry, at a time when rigidity, conformity and memorization were the norm. Weil was held in high regard by her students but her unconventional approach to educational life earned a reprimand from the superintendent of instruction, who threatened to revoke her teacher's license.

James D. Kirylo (Ed.), A Critical Pedagogy of Resistance: 34 Pedagogues We Need to Know, 129–132.

Weil's political convictions were further honed by the nine months she spent working in an automobile factory in her mid-twenties. In the years preceding this experience, she had already participated on picket lines, joined the unemployed in pick and shovel work, and given money, food and books to workers and the poor. Her factory experience halted by illness, she went on to support the Loyalists in the Spanish Civil War. Her time in Spain ended abruptly following an accident with cooking oil and she was taken by her parents to a hospital in Portugal to recover.

Weil moved to Marseille and became increasingly interested in questions of spirituality. Her views were shaped by the lay theologian Gustave Thibon, with whom she worked in French vineyards, and the Catholic priest Father Perrin. While sympathetic to Christianity, she did not want to join the Church. During this period, Nazi persecution saw her family seeking exile in New York. Weil, however, returned to London, with a view to joining the Free French forces against the Nazi occupation. As it turned out, she would never make it back to France, dying in August 1943 as a result of both tuberculosis and self-imposed nutritional restrictions. Principled to the end, and perhaps also suffering from anorexia nervosa, Weil had allowed herself only as much food as she felt would be available to those fighting in occupied France.

CRITICAL WRITINGS

Weil published little in her lifetime but after her death the notebooks she had kept and the letters she had written served as the basis for a number of posthumously published works, among the best known of which are *Gravity and Grace* (Weil, 1997) and *Waiting for God* (Weil, 2001a). Weil's corpus also includes *Oppression and Liberty* (Weil, 2001b), a key work on politics, and *The Need for Roots* (Weil, 2002), a plan for social renewal commissioned by the Free French in London. Weil's musings in other domains, including Homeric studies (Weil, 2005), literature, science and mathematics (Weil, 1968), and philosophy (Weil, 1978) are also available in print. In *Waiting for God*, there is an essay directly devoted to school studies, but the relevance of Weil's thought for education goes well beyond this source. Given space constraints, just a few points of particular significance for critical pedagogy will be highlighted here.

At the heart of Weil's philosophy of education is the notion of *attention* (Roberts, 2011; Smith, 2001; von der Ruhr, 2006). For Weil, attention means 'suspending our thought, leaving it detached, empty, and ready to be penetrated by the object' (2001a, p. 62). Attention requires openness, humility, a certain degree of detachment, and patience. Attention has ontological, epistemological and ethical import. As a mode of being, it stands opposed to the dominant contemporary construction of citizens as relentless consumers. We can come to know how to pay attention, even where we feel our progress in acquiring knowledge in a particular subject is less than ideal. The value of such effort will sometimes only be realized later in life. Perhaps most importantly, attention involves a turning away from the self – Weil (1997) calls this process *decreation* – with a view to caring for the Other. What those who suffer need most, Weil claims, is attention. Attention is thus closely connected with *love* (cf. Liston, 2008; Murdoch, 2001): the capacity to comprehend one's neighbor in all his or her fullness and to ask, "What are you going through?" (Weil, 2001a, p. 64).

From Weil we can learn that critical pedagogy entails utter devotion: to the students with whom one works, the process of study, and ongoing work on oneself. We tend to avoid that which is difficult – falling prey to *gravity*, as Weil (1997) terms it – and there is much in today's world that encourages us to take the easier path. Weil herself experienced a 'dark night of the soul' (Kovitz, 1992), but she showed that this is sometimes necessary if grace is to be bestowed upon us. We need not think of this purely in spiritual terms: grace arises in the unexpected moments of joy and fulfillment that emerge through our involvement as teachers in the lives of others. Weil reminds us that education is wonderfully unpredictable; she provides a clear counter to the obsession with measurement and performance that defines our current age.

Weil's attempts to assist others were not always successful, but in her earnestness and the sacrifices she made, she provides an example for others who seek to integrate theory with practice. Weil's work demonstrates that education will often be an uncomfortable process; it demands of us that we be open to questioning all that we hold dear. Calmness, listening and waiting are vital but so are passion and fortitude. Education is an inherently *risky* process and committing to it requires great courage. Had Simone Weil lived for another fifty years, there is no doubt she would have had a good deal more to say about teaching and learning. In the words and deeds that characterized her short life, however, there is much that is worthy of our ongoing attention.

REFERENCES

Fielder, L. (2001). Introduction. In: S. Weil, *Waiting for God* (vii–xxxiv). New York: Perennial Classics.
Kovitz, S. (1992). Simone Weil's dark night of the soul. *The Midwest Quarterly, 33*(3), 261–275.
Liston, D. P. (2008). Critical pedagogy and attentive love. *Studies in Philosophy and Education, 27*(5), 387–392.
McLellan, D. (1990). *Utopian pessimist: The life and thought of Simone Weil.* New York: Poseidon Press.
Murdoch, I. (2001). *The sovereignty of good.* London and New York: Routledge.
Roberts, P. (2011). Attention, asceticism, and grace: Simone Weil and higher education. *Arts and Humanities in Higher Education, 10*(3), 315–328.
Smith, R. (2001). Simone Weil (1909–1943). In J. Palmer (Ed.), *Fifty key educational thinkers.* London: Routledge.
von der Ruhr, M. (2006). *Simone Weil: An apprenticeship in attention.* London and New York: Continuum.
Weil, S. (1968). *On science, necessity, and the love of God* (R. Rees, Trans.). London: Oxford University Press.
Weil, S. (1978). *Lectures on philosophy* (H. Price, Trans.). Cambridge: Cambridge University Press.
Weil, S. (1997). *Gravity and grace* (A. Wills, Trans.). Lincoln: Bison Books.
Weil, S. (2001a). *Waiting for God* (E. Craufurd, Trans.). New York: Perennial Classics.
Weil, S. (2001b). *Oppression and liberty* (A. Wills & J. Petrie, Trans.). London and New York: Routledge Classics.
Weil, S. (2002). *The need for roots* (A. Wills, Trans.). London and New York: Routledge Classics.
Weil, S. (2005). The *Iliad*, or the poem of force. In S. Weil & R. Bespaloff, *War and the Iliad* (M. McCarthy, Trans.). New York: New York Review of Books.

34. CORNEL R. WEST

An Intellectual Soul of Justice and Compassion

> To be human you must bear witness to justice. Justice is what love looks like
> in public—to be human is to love and be loved.
>
> West, 2008, p. 181

Educator, philosopher, and Christian activist Cornel R. West (2008) describes
himself as man "cut against the grain" (p. 70). Holding the rare status of both a
Harvard and Princeton alumnus, West embodies the work of a passionate scholar,
voracious reader, and critical pedagogue. He is inspired by the magic and tradition of
myriad melodies of music. Paulo Freire (1998) reminds us that a central ingredient
of critical pedagogy is radical love, which implies movement toward freedom. It is
in the vain of being influenced by the work of Freire, that a radical love permeates
West's work (Kirylo, 2011).

EARLY LIFE AND EDUCATION

Born in Oklahoma but reared in California, Cornel West—"Corn" for short—grew
up close to and in the shadow of his older brother Cliff. In his younger years, his
family called him Ronnie, as Ronald is his middle name. Even at a young age, West
demonstrated resistant tendencies; as a third grader, he refused to recite the Pledge
of Allegiance. Because of this protest, he was: slapped by the teacher; paddled by
the principal; and forced to face his parents once he arrived home. Although West
claimed what he did what was right, his mother— who served as a former teacher
and principal—cried about the episode. His father gave him a whipping. Only his
brother Cliff consoled and attempted to reason with him.

An admitted inner bully resided inside West, but to some, it appeared as if a
"Robin Hood" mythological figure drove his thinking. While this inner-gnawing
rage infiltrated his being, he was tempered by his abilities as a voracious reader and
a brilliant violinist. As if that were not impressive enough, he spent his spare time
sharpening his skills as a track star. West's parents realized that their son was multi-
gifted, so they moved to Sacramento, California in an attempt to provide the best
opportunities—not only for him—for all their children. A significant life-changing
episode occurred when his pastor, Willie P. Cooke, baptized Cornel. On that special

James D. Kirylo (Ed.), A Critical Pedagogy of Resistance: 34 Pedagogues We Need to Know, 133–136.

day, his grandfather prayed over his grandson, prompting a transcendent, sacred event that seemingly transformed his rage. To keep Corn challenged, they encouraged him to continue reading and they also tried to make sure he had the best teachers at John F. Kennedy High School. West graduated at the top of his high school senior class and went on to study at Harvard. There he matriculated through his undergraduate program in only three years.

Three foundational components frame West's constitution: family, a Socratic spirituality in pursuit of truth, and his Christian commitment to the principles of love and justice. Overlaying that constitution, music of every genre is part and parcel to his being, particularly lit by the artistry of John Coltrane (West, 2009).

EDUCATIONAL CAREER

Shortly after his studies at Harvard, West joined the faculty at Union Theological Seminary in New York. He remained there for eight years. Later he enrolled at Princeton. West focused his dissertation research on the ethical aspects of Marxism and liberation theology and how these theories linked to Christ's love for people in poverty and to the social, economic, and political arenas of life. As a basis for his research agenda, the spirit of West's dissertation became the heart and soul of his life. West argued that while Karl Marx focused on concepts related to economics and the life of the proletariat, Marx maintained a social and spiritual perspective of Lutheranism. For West, Christianity and his love for music, coupled with critical philosophical and ethical constructs would constructively impact social conditions for human beings, especially people in poverty and of color (hooks & West; West, 2001).

After completing his studies at Princeton, West proceeded to teach at Harvard. Because of a fracture with the administration at Harvard, he taught for a short while at Yale. Eventually, West landed a teaching post in the African American Studies Center at Princeton. It stands to reason that West's association with James H. Cone and James Washington at Union Theological Seminary strongly influenced his blend of Christianity and social justice. These series of events certainly motivated him to maintain his association with Union Theological Seminary (West, 2009). Indeed, West recently returned to Union Theological Seminary in New York as Professor of philosophy and Christian practice in 2012.

DIVERSE MORAL COMPASS

In his best-selling book, *Race Matters* (1993), which was released following the one-year anniversary of the Rodney King police beating in Los Angeles, California, West argued the largely male, justified indignation that took place following the verdict could be characterized as "social rage" (p. 3). West cogently recounted historical and sociological prevalent perspectives among Caucasians toward African Americans, and particularly underscored the oppressive forces at work projected onto African

American males, specifically males of lower economic strati. Ultimately, the purpose of *Race Matters* was West's desire to revive a conversation about race, forcing a discourse that drew attention to how democratic ideals are being woefully undermined, and how legislation has particularly eroded voting rights for people of poverty and color.

In fact, West argues democracy is in a state of struggle—a time of crises—by the power structures particularly dominated by imperialistic, patriarchal, and white supremacy forces (hooks & West, 1991; West 1993; Taylor 2009). Despite myriad legislation, of course *The Declaration of Independence*, even in this era, Indigenous American Indians, Latinos, people of African and Asian descent, combined with the subordination and oppression of women, people in the working class, and of and gender identity and orientation are often subjugated. West (2001) compellingly makes the case of how freedoms have been historically denied, which has systematically created social and racial divides.

Cornel West and Tavis Smiley in *The Rich and The Rest of Us: A Poverty Manifesto* (2012) reiterates how the countless faces of power and wealth require transparency and truth. Wealth is uncontrolled, hiding behind tax loopholes and oppressing the middle and lower classes. That is, 42% of the wealth in the United States is regulated by 1% of the population, clearly implying that wealth has a monumental influence on elections. The very idea of democracy is disturbingly compromised. In other words, the voices of people in poverty and hunger—with numbers rapidly increasing in size—are virtually silenced in the existing social and economic reality. Most people are kept from full participation in a so-called democracy that presumably exists in the United States.

Passionate in his beliefs on the subject, West was not only a powerful force during the "Occupy" movement, he and Smiley also traveled a broad circuit attempting to alert the public about the issues of poverty and of the growing under classes in the United States. They sent a clear message that an unethical struggle exists between the "haves" and "have-nots." While traveling and talking with people from all backgrounds and ethnicities, West and Smiley interacted among people experiencing economic struggles, hunger, while living in tent cities, sleeping in vehicles, and that have been irrevocably harmed by self-serving economic policies. They go on to argue that the wealthy have demolished the American dream, creating an American nightmare, which now includes one-third of the American middle class now living in poverty (Smiley & West, 2012).

Smiley and West make it abundantly clear that poverty is often a hidden issue in the electoral process, further marginalizing the poor while at the same time the wealthiest of investors, lobbyists, and big businesses dominate the direction of political campaigns, and, indeed, the elections themselves. In that light, they desperately call for a deep, wide-awake rescue of democracy that is comprised of an authentic democratic process that includes the voices of the poor and the declining middle class, and where elections are not for sale (Smiley & West, 2012; Marable, 2006).

CONCLUSION

As one carefully examines West's work and life, it becomes transparent and apparent that he is dedicated and devoted to democratic social redistribution of wealth, power, education and human rights (Fraser, 1997; North, 2008). Social justice is the soul of West's (2008) coined phrase, "deep democracy – the courage to lift our voices and have them heard in order to shape our destiny" (p. 222). It is in every sense of the sum of the aforementioned, Cornel R. West lives and breathes to foster a world that is more just, more loving, and more hopeful, in his holistic effort to make a democratic meaningful alliance with every person regardless of the ethnic, race, language, and socio-economic background (Darder, Baltodano, & Torres, 2009; Fraser, 1997; North, 2008; West, 2008).

REFERENCES

Darder, A, Baltodano, M. P., & Torres, R. D. (Eds.). (2009). *The critical pedagogy reader.* New York, Routledge.

Fraser, N. (1997). *Justice interruptus: Critical reflections on the "postsocialist" condition.* New York: Routledge.

Freire, P. (1998). *Pedagogy of freedom: Ethics, democracy and civic courage.* Lanham, MD: Rowman and Littlefield Publishers, Inc.

Kirylo, J. D. (2011). *Paulo Freire: The man from Recife.* New York: Peter Lang.

Marable, M. (2006). *Living Black history: How reimagining the African American past can remake American's racial future.* New York: Basic Civitas Books.

North, C. (2008). What is all this talk about "Social Justice"? Mapping the terrain of education's latest catchphrase. *Teachers College Record, 110*(6), 1182–1206.

Smiley, T., & West, C. R. (2012). *The rich and the rest of us: A poverty manifesto.* New York: SmileyBooks.

Taylor, A. (2009). *Examined life: Excursions with contemporary thinkers.* New York: The New Press.

Watkins, G., (hooks, b.) & West, C. (1991). *Breaking bread: Insurgent black intellectual life.* Boston, MA: South End Press.

West, C. with Ritz, D. (2009). *Brother West: Living and loving out loud, a memoir.* New York: SmileyBooks.

West, C. (2001). *Cornel West: A Critical Reader.* New York: Civitas.

West, C. (2008). *Hope on a tightrope.* New York: SmileyBooks.

West, C. R. (1993). *Race matters.* Boston: Beacon Press.

CONTRIBUTORS

Jerry Aldridge is Professor Emeritus in early childhood education at the University of Alabama at Birmingham and a representative for the World Organization for Early Childhood Education (OMEP) to the United Nations. He has published over 200 articles and 12 books. Co-authored with Lois M. Christensen, his latest book is titled *Critical Pedagogy for Early Childhood and Elementary Educators*.

Gerlinde Beckers is an assistant professor of literacy in the College of Education at Southeastern Louisiana University. In addition to her deep interest in the work of Deborah Britzman, her research also focuses on struggling adolescent readers and literacy as a social responsibility. She has worked many years in the field of education from early elementary to postsecondary level.

Marika Barto is a Ph.D. candidate at the University of New Orleans, and is a social justice educator. She is currently studying social justice curriculum models and their impact on the school-to-prison pipeline. Marika has been a high school science teacher, director of a residential boys' home, and assistant principal of a charter school in New Orleans.

April Whatley Bedford is a Professor and Interim Dean of the College of Education and Human Development at the University of New Orleans. Her teaching and scholarship have focused on children's literature, early literacy, and teacher development.

Renée Casbergue holds the Vira Franklin and James R. Eagle Professorship at Louisiana State University where she serves as Associate Dean for Graduate Studies and Research. She teaches graduate literacy courses and works with the early childhood teacher certification program. Her research focuses on early literacy and preschool teachers' professional development.

Basanti D. Chakraborty is an Associate Professor of Early Childhood Education at New Jersey City University. She serves on the publication committee of the Association for Childhood Education International and co-edits the Idea Sparkers column. She is an active advocate of children and women who partners with advocacy groups internationally. Her research interests focus on issues related to equity and fairness in education. In addition to authoring *Education of the Creative Children* (Konark Publishers, India), Chakraborty has written a number of book chapters and articles in education.

Lois McFadyen Christensen is Professor of Curriculum and Instruction in the School of Education at the University of Alabama at Birmingham. Her publications and presentations particularly pertain to social studies – social justice, Reggio Emilia inspired approaches, critical pedagogy, women's issues, and qualitative methods.

James D. Kirylo (Ed.), A Critical Pedagogy of Resistance: 34 Pedagogues We Need to Know, 137–142.
© 2013 Sense Publishers. All rights reserved.

William Crain is a Professor of Psychology at The City College of The City University of New York. He is the author of *Reclaiming Childhood: Letting Children Be Children in Our Achievement-Oriented Society* and the textbook, *Theories of Development: Concepts and Applications*, now in its sixth edition. A political activist, Crain is engaged in the effort to keep The City University accessible to working class students and students of color. He also is active in the defense of nature.

Patricia A. Crawford is an Associate Professor at the University of Pittsburgh, where she works with practicing and prospective teachers, as well as emerging researchers. She serves as the associate chairperson for the Department of Instruction and Learning, and teaches across the areas of early childhood and literacy education.

Lynda Robbirds Daughenbaugh is Associate Professor of elementary reading and literature courses in the Leadership and Teacher Education Department at the University of South Alabama, Mobile, Alabama.

Chandni Desai is a doctoral student at the Ontario Institute for Studies in Education of the University of Toronto. Her research interests include cultural and political resistance in Israel-Palestine, Hip Hop education, decolonizing education, and critical race theory.

Betty T. Dlamini is a senior lecturer and current Dean of the Faculty of education at the University of Swaziland. She specializes in science education, and her research also includes examining classroom practice. Dlamini is the author of numerous articles and book chapters.

Takisha Durm is a doctoral student in the curriculum and instruction program in the College of Education at The University of Alabama. Her research interests focus on social justice curricula, African American male achievement, and service learning programs for marginalized youth.

John Fischetti is Dean and Professor in the College of Education at Southeastern Louisiana University in Hammond. His research focuses on school reform, equity, school leadership and curriculum that promotes student learning. Fischetti's commitment is assisting public schools in fulfilling their mission to improve the human condition.

Rubén A. Gaztambide-Fernández is an Associate Professor at the Ontario Institute for Studies in Education of the University of Toronto. His research focuses on the social context of cultural production and on processes of identification in schools. He is the author of *The Best of the Best: Becoming Elite at an American Boarding School* (2009, Harvard University Press).

Kathy Fite is a professor at Texas State University. She is an active researcher, author, speaker, and advocate of early childhood education, and has worked with preschoolers to doctoral-level students. She is on the advisory council for the Gesell Institute for Child Development and on the board for the Association for Childhood Education International.

Aino Hannula is a lecturer for the School of Teacher Education at the University of Eastern Finland. Her research interests focuses on Freirean pedagogy, community education and social life in class rooms. She has worked for many years in the area of education and psychology.

John Kambutu is an Associate Professor and Department Head of Educational Studies at the University of Wyoming/Casper College Center. His research work is in cultural diversity, rural education, and transformative learning. He also has scholarly interest in globalization/internationalization efforts.

Jennifer L. Kilgo is University Professor of early intervention/early childhood special education at the University of Alabama at Birmingham (UAB). She has received numerous federally funded grants and served in a number of national leadership positions including President of the Division for Early Childhood (DEC) of the Council for Exceptional Children (CEC). She has authored or co-authored many journal articles, chapters, and books. Kilgo's most recent book, *An Introduction to Young Children with Special Needs: Birth Through Age Eight* (with Richard Gargiulo), was published in its 4th edition.

James D. Kirylo is Associate Professor of Education in the College of Education and Human Development at Southeastern Louisiana University. His research interests are in the areas of critical pedagogy, teacher leadership, curriculum theory, and literacy. He is the author of *Paulo Freire: The Man from Recife* (2011, Peter Lang), and co-editor for the book *Curriculum Development: Perspectives from Around the World* (2010, ACEI).

Ann Larson currently serves as Vice Dean and is a Professor in the Department of Middle and Secondary Education, College of Education and Human Development at the University of Louisville, Louisville, Kentucky. Her publications typically appear in teacher education and foundations of education journals.

Michael E. Lee is Associate Professor of Systematic Theology at Fordham University in New York City, and member of its Latin American and Latino Studies Institute. He received his Ph.D. in Theology from the University of Notre Dame. He has published *Bearing the Weight of Salvation: The Soteriology of Ignacio Ellacuría* (NY: Crossroad, 2009), and is the editor for the book *Ellacuría: Essays on History, Liberation and Salvation* (Maryknoll, NY: Orbis Books, 2013).

Jan Lacina is Associate Dean of Graduate Studies in the College of Education at Texas Christian University in Fort Worth, Texas. She is the author of more than 60 publications, including three books. She is currently serving as Editor for the Journal of Research in Childhood Education (JRCE).

Tondra Loder-Jackson is an Associate Professor in the School of Education and Director of the Center for Urban Education at The University of Alabama at Birmingham. She is currently writing a book on African American educators' contributions to the Birmingham Civil Rights Movement and contemporary urban education.

Luis Mirón is Dean of the College of Social Sciences at Loyola University New Orleans. An internationally recognized scholar, Mirón is the author of numerous articles and is the author/co-author of several books, including *The Social Construction of Urban Schooling* (1996 Hampton); *Resisting Discrimination: Affirmative Strategies for Principals and Teachers* (1996, Corwin); *Race, Identity, and Citizenship: A Reader* (1999, Wiley-Blackwell); and *Reinterpreting Urban School Reform: Have Urban Schools Failed, or Has the Reform Movement Failed Urban Schools?(State University of New York Press, 2003)*.

Gabriel Morley earned his doctorate in adult education from The University of Southern Mississippi. His research focuses on informal learning, especially among the counterculture. His dissertation analyzed hippy adult educator Stephen Gaskin and his unique approach to emancipatory learning through psychedelic drugs, spirituality, and ecological consciousness.

Lydiah Nganga is an Associate Professor of Elementary and Early Childhood Education at the University of Wyoming/Casper College Center. Her research work is in cultural diversity, social justice, rural education and global educational issues. She also possesses a scholarly interest in international comparative education and early childhood education.

Kennedy Ongaga is an Assistant Professor in the Department of Educational Leadership at the University of North Carolina Wilmington. His research focuses on educational reform, educational administration, small learning communities, and issues of social justice in education.

Debra Panizzon holds the position of Associate Professor in the School of Education at Monash University in Melbourne, Australia. An experienced science education academic having worked with primary and secondary school preservice teachers, Debra has diverse research interests in the areas of cognition, student acquisition of scientific concepts, rural and regional education, and assessment.

Linda Pickett is an Associate Professor and Coordinator of the Early Childhood Education Department at Grand Valley State University. She studied multicultural education at the University of New Mexico and taught in kindergarten through 2nd grade classrooms. Her recent scholarship has focused on Integrated Education in Northern Ireland, diversity and transformations of US classrooms to promote education for peace and social justice.

Cole Reilly is an Assistant Professor at Towson University, where he teaches curricular and pedagogical methods courses to preservice and practicing K-12 educators. His scholarly interests draw upon feminist pedagogies and curricular (re)design, as well as social constructivist meaning making around notions of gender(ing), sexuality, race, and/or class structures.

Peter Roberts is Professor of Education at the University of Canterbury in New Zealand. His primary areas of scholarship are philosophy of education and educational policy studies. His research interests include the ethics and politics of education, the pedagogy of Paulo Freire, literature and education, and tertiary education policy.

Janna Siegel Robertson has worked in the field of education for 30 years. She is currently a Professor of Secondary Education at the University of North Carolina, Wilmington. Her research focuses in the areas of dropout prevention, at-risk students, instructional technology, teacher preparation, arts education, and diverse populations.

Arturo Rodriguez is Associate Professor of Bilingual Education at Boise State University. He earned a Ph.D. in Language, Literacy and Culture at New Mexico State University in 2006. A former high school teacher, his research interests include critical theory/pedagogy, intercultural and democratic education and education for social justice.

Jovita M. Ross-Gordon is a Professor of Adult, Professional and Community Education at Texas State University where she coordinates the MA in Adult Education. She has authored numerous books, chapters and articles on teaching and learning of adults. She is Co-Editor of Adult *Education Quarterly and of New Directions for Adult and Continuing Education.*

Edward L. Shaw, Jr. is a Professor of Elementary Science Education at the University of South Alabama, Mobile, AL.

Kris Sloan is an Associate Professor in the School of Education at St. Edward's University in Austin, Texas. He teaches courses on culture, curriculum, and educational policy at both the graduate and undergraduate levels. Sloan has published works on anti-oppressive education, educational policy, accountability, and assessment literacy.

Matthew David Smith completed his Ph.D. under Peter McLaren. Matthew came to critical pedagogy via his teaching and learning in bilingual education. He began his teaching career in Albuquerque, New Mexico, and completed his undergraduate and Masters' degree at the University of New Mexico.

Sandra J. Stone, a well-known author and speaker, is a Professor at Northern Arizona University. She founded and directs the National Multiage Institute. Her research interests include multiage education, literacy, and play. Among her many published works are the books *Creating the Multiage Classroom* and *Playing: A Kid's Curriculum.*

Tunde Szecsi is an Associate Professor at Florida Gulf Coast University, Fort Myers. She earned her Master's degrees in Hungary, and her Ph.D. in Early Childhood Education at the University at Buffalo. Both in English and Hungarian, she has published articles and has made presentations on culturally responsive teacher preparation, and heritage language learning.

Cristina P. Valentino graduated from the University of North Florida with a degree in Educational Leadership with concentration in ESOL-ESL/Multicultural-Bilingual Education/Language Acquisition. She has conducted postdoctoral research on bilingual giftedness in Honduras and conducted workshops from Population Connection in the U.S. and Honduras. She has served as a program reviewer for the Florida Department of Education.

Elizabeth Wadlington is a Professor at Southeastern Louisiana University. Possessing a special interest in John Dewey's philosophy and modern applications, Wadlington currently teaches and researches in the areas of literacy, dyslexia, English as a Second Language, and teacher and student dispositions.

Debora B. Wisneski is an associate professor in early childhood education at the University of Nebraska at Omaha. Her research interests include qualitative research exploring classroom community through play and story. She is past President of the Association for Childhood Education International.

CPSIA information can be obtained at www.ICGtesting.com
Printed in the USA
BVOW11s1016180814

363275BV00010B/601/P